To Love
To Betray

Other books by Aldo Carotenuto

A Secret Symmetry: Sabina Spielrein Between Jung and Freud
The Vertical Labyrinth: Individuation in Jungian Psychology
The Spiral Way: A Woman's Healing Journey
Eros and Pathos: Shades of Love and Suffering
Kant's Dove: The History of Transference in Psychoanalysis
The Difficult Art: A Critical Discourse on Psychotherapy
The Call of the Daimon: Love and Truth in the Writings
    of Franz Kafka—The Trial and the Castle

To Love
To Betray

Life as Betrayal

Aldo Carotenuto

Translated by
Joan Tambureno

Chiron Publications • Wilmette, Illinois

Originally published in Italian in 1991 as *Amare Tradire*.
© 1991, Gruppo Editoriale Fabbri, Bompiani, Sonzogno, Etas S. p. A. Milan.

English translation prepared for Aldo Carotenuto by Joan Tambureno.

Library of Congress Catalog Card Number: 95-51849

Printed in the United States of America.
Copyedited by Carla Babrick.
Book design by Ellen Scanlon.
Cover design by D. J. Hyde.

Library of Congress Cataloging-in-Publication Data:

Carotenuto, Aldo, 1933–
 [Amare tradire. English]
 To love, to betray : life as betrayal / Aldo Carotenuto : translated by Joan Tambureno.
  p. cm.
 Includes bibliographical references and index.
 ISBN 0-933029-97-7 (trade paperback)
  1. Psychic trauma. 2. Betrayal—Psychological aspects. 3. Trust (psychology) 4. Jungian psychology. I. Title.
 BF175.5.P75C3713 1996
 155.9′2—dc20   95-51849
                                                                        CIP

ISBN 0-933029-97-7

Contents

Chapter

Acknowledgments

My decision to address so particular a subject was the logical consequence of encounters with individuals who, unknowingly, contributed to certain reflections. In that context, I should like to express my sincerest thanks to my students and assistants Francesca Aveni, Daniela Bucelli, Simonetta Massa, Benedetta Silj, and Stefania Tucci for having helped resolve those endless problems which arise during the production of any book. Special thanks as well to my students Giorgio Antonelli, Silvia Martufi, and Patrizia Lorenzi who kindly read my notes and provided precious criticism and suggestions.

Introduction

Life as Betrayal

Yet I will remember the favours of these men.
Were they not mine?
Did they not sometimes cry "All Hail!" to me?
So Judas did to Christ;
But he in twelve, found truth in all but one;
I, in twelve thousand, none.
———Shakespeare, *Richard II*

My book *Eros and Pathos* (1987) dealt with the dimension of love, one of the fundamental aspects of human life. I wrote that book fully aware that I was venturing into a sphere usually considered inaccessible, since the most authentic expression of certain ineffable experiences would probably be silence. However, with the same awareness—and the same assurance—I have taken a similarly difficult path to explore one of the most disturbing aspects of human experience: betrayal.

Terrible, infamous word! And yet, on closer examination, we must draw the surprising conclusion that not only is betrayal a constant presence in our lives—in an important if not fundamental role—but within the Christian worldview expressed in the book of Genesis, it is as a direct result of betrayal that human beings were brought into the world. The betrayal described in Genesis was an inevitable and necessarily total one because only thus, by breaking the original pact with God, could human beings—whose natural state was not life, but unconsciousness and nondifferentiation—become protagonists.

This betrayal is the underlying sense of the doctrine of *felix culpa*, which links the redemption of Christ's coming (and consequently, the possibility of our redemption and new life) to the original sin of Adam and Eve. In other words, if our mythical progenitors had not sinned, Christ obviously would not have appeared on earth on his mission of redemption; redemption presupposes the existence of sin. Thus, we are born into the world only through sin.

The doctrine of *felix culpa* is also present in Hegel's concept of the myth of original sin as an "upward falling." And, in the context of recovery and redefinition of the original betrayal, Gnostic doctrine—according to which what should really be venerated is the knowledge (gnosis)-transmitting serpent of Eden—appears legitimate as well. That transmission of knowledge could be equated with the possibility of seeing life, all life, as betrayal. We might keep in mind the foundations of the Jewish and Christian religions: the original sin of Adam and Eve in the Old Testament and Christ's betrayal by Judas in the New. Actually, the entire Old Testament, which the Gnostics considered the manifest expression of divine betrayal, could be just as well interpreted as the eternal message of God betrayed by Israel: the "unfaithful spouse," the "Whore" whom He nevertheless ceaselessly seeks. Also consider the passage from the prophet Hosea, in which the past and present of Israel are synthesized using the concept of betrayal:

> But they like men have transgressed the covenant: there have they dealt treacherously against me. (Hosea 6.7 King James Version)

And as Hillman (1964b, 64) wrote:

> Since the expulsion, the Bible records a history of betrayals of many sorts. Cain and Abel, Jacob and Esau, Laban, Joseph sold by his brothers and their father deceived, Pharaoh's broken promises, calf-worship behind Moses' back, Saul, Samson, Job, God's rages and the creation almost annulled—on and on, culminating in the central myth of our culture: the betrayal of Jesus.

Yet, such is the mystery of betrayal that, according to the Talmud, had Israel not been soiled by her crimes, sins, and betrayals, God would have given that nation only the books of the

Pentateuch (the laws of Moses) and the book of Joshua (Talmud, Nedarim 22b, in Elkaim-Sartre 1982). Analogously, in the New Testament, it is not only Judas who betrays. Certainly, his act would appear to be the height of betrayal, and in this sense Kierkegaard would have agreed with Hillman: Kierkegaard noted in his diary that to truly penetrate the Christianity of an age, it is sufficient to observe its concept of Judas (1834–1855). However, other betrayals in the New Testament could be considered equally significant; the denial of Peter, for example, or the disciples' falling asleep in the Garden of Gethsemane. And could we not also interpret Christ's dying cry to the heavens—"My God, my God, why hast thou forsaken me?" (Matthew 27.46)—as the ultimate betrayal of the Father?

Omnipresent in myth and sacred texts, betrayal has also permeated profane history with its unsettling quality. Julien Benda, in his famous work published in 1927, referred to a "betrayal of the clergy." His theory was that, if the role of the intellectual was to preserve universal values—in the service of truth, justice, reason, and individual liberty—then intellectuals had betrayed their historical and, inevitably, metahistorical mission. The clergy placed art and science at the service of political and economic interests, adhering to the suppression of the individual while exalting the monolithic state, extolling the family—which negates the individual—as a comprehensive organism, and harboring sympathy for corporatism. The clergy failed to place the concept of peace above all, giving in to ideologies and, through the doctrines of those ideologies, indulging in political passions. Benda noted that in various ways and in the name of order, commitment, love, the sacred nature of the writer, the relativism of good and evil, and communion with evolution and world dynamism—a communion that translates into measuring change not according to reason but vitalist adherence—the intellectuals have perpetrated their betrayal. And we could at this point introduce other betrayals that, from the depths of myth, sacred and profane history, and all the "great systems," plunged their blade into the labyrinthine commonplace; in other words, betrayals with which that other intellectual—the psychoanalyst—must constantly deal.

Therefore, life—all life—can include betrayal. The earthly

paradise, intended as the plenitude and nondifferentiation of prenatal life, was an untenable condition, since we were forced to betray it (through birth) when the world and history spread out before us. A metaphorical expression for what characterizes the human condition, or an expression of the real tragedy of man, might be the nonexistence of paradise. The Garden of Eden does not exist, and paradise is not of this world. Paradise is a dimension of nondualism, of nondesire and thus of nonattachment, a dimension in which the human heart is not agitated, because it is complete unto itself, where it knows no anticipation because it is fulfilled unto itself, and where it knows no fear of death because it is life. Paradise, therefore, understood as the overwhelming idea of plenitude, is not of this world.

According to Otto Rank, one of the great heretics of psychoanalysis, our lives are entirely spent in the attempt to substitute the paradise lost with extremely complicated changes in the direction and destination of our libidos (Rank 1924). Rank knew, in any case, that we will never again find that paradise lost. Consequently, the deduction could be made that those changes in the direction of the libido of which he speaks correspond to as many betrayals. In fact, if paradise is not earthly, betrayal is! And not even a god will avoid it. For, as Franco Sacchetti wrote, even Christ was betrayed (Sacchetti 1970).

One

Even Before Birth

And the voice of the Father came from the throne, say-
ing: "What are you doing, accursed one, you who cor-
rupt the angels? Author of sin, do quickly what you in-
tend."

—*Interrogatio Iohannis*

One of the discoveries resulting from Freud's studies on
dreams was that, as the unconscious excludes negation, consciousness of any representation of "no" is impossible in dreams.
Consequently, the same oneiric image must be valid for both affirmation and negation. That double movement could also be
applied to language, as Freud learned from a short study published in 1884 by the philologist Karl Abel on the opposite significance of primal words. Subsequently, Freud drew the conclusion that in the most ancient languages—above all, in Egyptian,
but in the Semitic and Indo-European languages as well—the
expression of opposites, such as "strong/weak" or "large/small,"
had the same linguistic root. Thus, he discovered an analogy between the history of language and that "strange behaviour of the
dreamwork" which excludes negation (Freud 1915–1917). In a
1910 review entitled *The Antithetical Meaning of Primal Words*
(in homage to Abel's study), Freud managed to cite numerous
examples to support this idea. "In Latin," he wrote, "*altus* means
'high' and 'deep,' *sacer* 'sacred' and 'accursed'" (Freud 1910,
159). In the concordance between the oneiric and the linguistic,
Freud found confirmation of "the view we have formed about
the regressive archaic character of the expression of thoughts
in dreams." The review concluded with the assertion that

knowledge of the evolution of language in general would certainly improve the understanding and interpretation of oneiric language (ibid., 161).

Similar observations can be made regarding the word *betrayal*. In fact, on closer examination, the word appears ambiguous, in both the etymological and the semantic sense. We know that the Latin *tradere* signifies only "to consign." We also know that that verb, used in the gospel to describe the act of Judas in delivering Jesus to his enemies, was loaded with ethical, and obviously negative, connotations. With time, the initial misunderstanding generated subsequent misunderstandings and ambiguities: the semantic itinerary of this "damned" and "condemned" verb included stopping-off points often considerably removed from one another; at times antipodal, literally opposite. *I betray* is derived from the Latin *trado*, and *trado* is composed of two morphemes, *trans* and *do* ("give").

The prefix *trans* implies a passage and, in fact, the original meanings of *trado* have everything to do with the giving of something, something passing from hand to hand. *Trado* can thus mean the act of consigning (in custody, for protection or punishment); the act of entrusting for command or instruction; the act of giving in matrimony; and selling, entrusting verbally, handing or passing down, or recounting. In the reflexive form, the verb *se tradere* means abandoning oneself to someone, dedicating oneself to some activity. The meanings of the corresponding substantive *traditio* are "consignment, instruction, recounting, the handing down of tales," and "tradition." In this sense, it is interesting to note that the *nomen agentis traditor* can mean either "traitor" or "he who instructs." Note also that duplicity in the introduction of this book since, as we will see further on, betrayal has something to teach us—perhaps only those who betray in total awareness. As Hillman (1964b, 76) observed:

> *the capacity to betray others is akin to the capacity to lead others.*

As a matter of fact, *to betray* came in time to mean the exact opposite, with the result that the original meaning was lost or, we might say, concealed. We might well ask how its initial positive connotation was changed to the present negative one. That inversion of meaning occurred in latinity and most probably originated in military language. The object of the original meaning of "passage" or "consignment," in fact, could have been the enemy, in which case it could connote the act of consigning arms, cities, or other things to the enemy, thus *tradendo*. I have already pointed out the affinities between the language of love and military language; in Latin the *nomen agentis desultor* connotes both he who goes from one woman to another—in the sense that Ovid (*Amores* I.3.15) denied being a traitor—as well as he who goes over to the enemy (Carotenuto 1990). The perfect equivalent of the Greek *I betray* is *paradidomi. Trans + do = para' + didomi.* And *paradidomi* is in fact the verb used in the gospel to describe the betrayal of Judas.

Note that the prefix *para*, like *trans*, can imply the act of "trans-gression" (or *para basis*, "going beyond, going over to the other side"). The corresponding substantive *paradosis*, the equivalent of *traditio*, means betrayal but also doctrine handed down authoritatively, or tradition truly preserved and separately transmitted by Pagans, scribes, and Pharisees (the predecessors of rabbis), by Paul and the bishops of the church.

For the Gnostics—those heretics of early Christianity—there existed a secret, oral doctrine which was transmitted by Christ to the apostles and which they considered superior to the Scriptures. Reference to that secret transmission—the act of which is indicated with the verb *paradidomi*—persists also in orthodox spheres. Clement of Alexandria, in *Stromati* (I.1.13.4) stated that "the hidden things" (Clement says "mystic") "are transmitted (*paradidotai*) in a concealed manner" (according to Clement, "in a mystical manner"). As for the Gnostics, they considered themselves the sole repositories of the true tradition. In fact, the early Church had to struggle against that claim. In the apocrypha according to Judas within the Gnostic literature, there also exists a "Mystery (Sacrament) of the Betrayal," revered by some Gnostic groups, according to which Judas' betrayal of Christ made salvation possible. Therefore, the Gnostics considered that betrayal as necessary and, as a consequence, observed it as a sacrament. According to other authors, Judas was aware that Christ was perverting—that is, betraying—the truth. By betraying Christ, Judas prevented Christ's own betrayal of the truth. Hillman, analogously, observed that betrayal was pertinent to Christianity (Hillman 1964b, 69):

> In the story of Jesus we are immediately struck by the motif of betrayal. Its occurrence in threes (by Judas, by the sleeping disciples, by Peter)—is repeated by Peter's betrayal thrice—tells us of something fateful; that betrayal is essential to the dynamics of the climax of the Jesus story and thus betrayal is at the heart of the Christian mystery.

However, Hillman continues, the same key can be used, as we have in part seen, to interpret other critical points in the earthly existence of Christ: his sadness during the Last Supper and in Gethsemane ("My soul is sick unto death"), and his lamentation from the cross ("My God, my God, why has thou abandoned me?"). In the last, tragic words of Christ's earthly existence, Jung saw the sign of devastating failure. According to a comment made by Jung during a conference held in London on October 19, 1936, intriguingly entitled, "Is Analytical Psychology a Religion?" (1937), Christ became aware, upon the cross and in proximity to the final passage, of the fact that his own life, which had been dedicated to truth and love, had been nothing more than a terrible illusion. Christ's cry from the cross, expressing the tragic realization of having been betrayed, thus justifies Jung's extreme criticism that Christ had never wondered about himself, never confronted himself (Jung 1952). Betrayal, therefore, forces us to look at ourselves. What is more, only through betrayal does that confrontation with ourselves, that ceasing to live in reflections not our own, become possible. Subsequently, we—like Jung—cannot escape having doubts about the Father (ibid., 398):

> What kind of father is it who would rather his son were slaughtered than forgive his ill-advised creatures who have been corrupted by his precious Satan?

And yet, that is the dialectic inherent in betrayal, in light of which it becomes possible to comprehend the painful meaning of faithfulness. Christ was abandoned to his agony on the cross and, consequently, betrayed—consigned (delivered unto) to the annihilation of that illusion which had sustained him during his earthly passage. But it is just that unquestioning faithfulness, that devoted loyalty, that fidelity to the experiment of life—as well as that faithfulness betrayed—which permitted the Resurrection of Christ (Jung 1937).

As we have seen, there would also have been space in the cogitative area of Gnosticism for the elaboration of the most radical aspects of betrayal: for example, the doctrine variously adhered to by the Gnostics which—by assigning the Creation of this world to an imperfect Demiurge, corresponding to the Hebrew Yahweh, and not to the Divine Being—contemplated in certain cases the inevitability of disobedience to—in other words, betrayal of—the Commandments. In fact, that doctrine includes a betrayal perpetrated even before we are born, but also its resolution.

In that same heretical context, consider the inversion of sign mentioned earlier that was undergone by the figure of the serpent in the context of a demiurgic and not exactly divine creation of the world of men. It is the evil serpent—or better still, Satan entered into the serpent—who slithers into Eden, preexistent to the creation of man and woman, to present Adam and Eve with the gift of knowledge through transgression, consequently constellating betrayal of the divine injunction against eating the prohibited fruit.

Consider also the revelation contained in the Coptic text entitled *The Hypostasis of the Archontes* (Erbetta 1982). This work was discovered in December 1945, together with numerous other documents, both Gnostic and others, at Nag' Hammadi in Upper Egypt. *Hypostasis* means "reality," the reality which subjects. The Archontes, dominators of the earthly world, whom Jung equated to complexes, are therefore real—malignantly real—beings. People who are incapable of transcending the Archontes become their slaves; in other words, those individuals are at risk who let themselves be betrayed by their perverse actions and who, thus betrayed, consign themselves to a destiny that is only apparently irreversible. The Gnostic scripture includes an esoteric interpretation of the passage from Genesis that is of considerable interest to us in the context of betrayal. In *The Hypostasis of the Archontes*, the instructor serpent says:

> "You will not die of death, for he has told you that out of envy.
> Instead, your eyes will be opened and you will be as the gods,
> knowing evil and good." . . . The woman took (it) from the tree,
> partook of it and thence gave it to her husband . . . .

In *Interrogatio Iohannis* (Bozoky 1980), the prospects of humanity's betrayal by the divinity acquire if anything even greater resonance. The *Interrogatio* is an apocrypha of Bogomil origin—that is, a text or catechism of sorts, part of the dualist heresy known as Bogomilismo which originated around the second half of the tenth century. That heresy conserved various points of contact with Gnosticism, and the text was one also referred to by several medieval heretic groups, one of which was the Cathari. In that text, the apostle John, reposing on Christ's breast, poses questions about Satan. In a subsequent tale, we are informed of a compromise of sorts between God and Satan, even before the creation of the world or of humans—a compromise that has an analogy in the Bible, in the Book of Job. After his Fall—the result of his desire to be elevated to the level of the Father, to become his equal—Satan descends from heaven to earth and there, together with his angels, failing to find peace, obtains it from the Father. According to the text, the Father permitted him to do what he would up until the seventh day (ibid.). The world is, therefore, the realm of Satan.

In fact, in the Gospel of John, reference is made to the "prince of this world." What disturbs, however, is the fact that in the version of the Bogomil heretics, the realm of Satan is to some extent favored by God. That is, before we were born, the drama of betrayal had already had its cosmological and mythological celebration. And, as noted, there had also been the resolution of that drama—obviously not a definitive one, but one which is manifest in the necessity that humanity (in the same way as Adam and Eve who introduced them) assume the weight of that drama. The fact that our forebears were cast "down onto the earth" after their transgression—or their betrayal of the pact made with God and the Demiurge—suggests the ulterior idea that the acquisition of the awareness of betrayal and, therefore—in the vision we are prepared to embrace—the acquisition of awareness *tout court*, inevitably passes through the elaboration of evil and inferiority.

The theme of inferiority brings us back to the observation on the figure of Judas made by Borges in his *Ficciones*. And, at this point, we might say that versions of the story of Judas are many. De Quincey was of the opinion that what was traditionally attributed to Judas was completely destitute of truth (Borges 1944). Borges refers to "three versions of Judas," referring to studies on the subject by Nils Runeberg, to whom (writes Borges) God assigned the twentieth century and the university city of Lund, but who in the Alexandria or Asia Minor of the second century would have directed with fervent intellectual passion one of the Gnostic conventicles (ibid.). One in particular of the three versions referred to by Borges deserves mention, one in which the problems of inferiority and betrayal appear to fuse and, thus fused, acquire divine significance. According to that version, it is God who chooses to be incarnated in Judas; God became man entirely, but to the point of infamy, to the point of damnation and the abyss. To save us, he could have chosen any one of the many destinies making up the complex web of history; he could have become Alexander or Pythagoras or Rurik or Jesus. Instead, he chose the lowest of destinies; he chose Judas (ibid.).

Therefore, we are confronted with betrayal in an antithetical and painfully dialectical way. Traces remain even in everyday language of the dialectical antithetical quality inherent in the semantics of betrayal. One example of this might be the translator's betrayal of an author's intentions, or an interviewer's betrayal of the person he interviews—in both cases, through distortion and misrepresentation. It would be equally legitimate to say that a person's secret thoughts can be betrayed by a gesture which reveals them, telling us the truth. Both falsehood and that which is authentic can betray. It is precisely this unsettling ambiguity that in a certain sense restores some of this verb's original neutral quality. And it is also this ambiguity which makes possible the affirmation that it is possible to "betray" without *betraying*; to break a pact, but in the name of a higher or deeper fidelity.

Two

A Fatal "Happy Event"

. . . where the swelling breast, the chancre.
          —M. Maier in Jung, *Mysterium Coniunctionis*

The experience of separation is the experience of life itself. Even the act of writing this book could be considered an example of dualism: Discourse is thought, and thought will inexorably reap a harvest of separation, division, and distance, revealing itself as an indescribable betrayal of immediate experience. An even more extreme example of this kind of betrayal is that presented by writing which blithely leads the reader into areas of the psyche not adequately experienced by the author. Apropos of this, Kierkegaard lamented the decadent state of writing: there are those, noted the great Danish philosopher in his extensive diary, who write on subjects upon which they have neither reflected nor experienced. He adds that as a consequence he has decided to read only the writings of men condemned to death or of those who have at least experienced real danger (Kierkegaard 1834–1855).

We might include the psychologist among the condemned men referred to by Kierkegaard. The reader is reminded once more, however, that the act of writing in itself can be betrayal. And that, paradoxically, is also—if not above all—true of writing electing betrayal as its object.

On the ontogenetic plane—on which the individual experiences those commonly shared passages essential to his evolution—it is at the moment of birth that each human being experiences betrayal for the first time. The word *betrayal* acquires an even more powerful emotional content when it involves the breaking of a pact; the pact between God and humanity in Genesis, the pact of human love and solidarity. If we have the courage to contemplate the darker side of life, we can even see birth as betrayal.

Birth is unquestionably a traumatic, even violent, event in the context of primary narcissism—that is, birth sunders the primary unit in which mother and child are contained, which Freud describes as having an "oceanic feeling" within the continuous flow of life. Moving out of this condition, through birth, causes mother and child to experience a fundamental separation anxiety. Birth is a terrible trauma for the child, who is mysteriously and arbitrarily expelled from that oceanic dimension. The loss, the interruption, the shattering of that symbiosis, constitutes an experience of anxiety which cannot be verbalized, formulated, or elaborated intellectually by the child. The child is in no position to describe this event, which is so totalizing as to permeate with its own unutterable nature one's entire existence and personality.

Otto Rank considered the birth trauma to be the decisive event in every existence, a primary experience powerful enough to shape destinies. From this viewpoint (proposed as all-inclusive), sexuality and myth, art, neurosis, conflict, and perversion all appear to have their origins in the decisive moment of detachment from the womb. Analysis itself is deeply bound to the birth trauma; in fact, Rank considered it to be its supplementary development (Rank 1924, 5). In what way? Rank observed that the unconscious represents the healing process through the symbolism of birth and—we might add—rebirth. The patient is born again as the spiritual child of the analyst and is thus delivered from the Oedipal fixation:

> He (the patient) does this finally by renouncing the phantasy of the infant child, which he—as the mother—wishes to present to the father, and by considering himself the new-born (spiritual) child (of the analyst) (ibid.).

Rank, in this context, speaks of the "anagogic nature of the phantasm of second birth." Consequently, true birth implies rebirth. Note that these concepts were included in Rank's *The*

Trauma of Birth (1924), which consummates his "betrayal" of Freud. In fact, in the chapter on analytical knowledge, he reveals himself as being completely aware of that problem—in particular, the passage in which he describes the disciple's emancipation from the master (ibid.). We might even say that *The Trauma of Birth*, in which Rank "betrays" Freud—or, in any case, starts in another direction—corresponds to Rank's own rebirth. Betraying, in other words, can constitute a way, if not the way, to rebirth. An analogous observation could perhaps be made regarding *Symbols of Transformation*, in which Jung also questions the "double birth of the hero." To borrow an expression from Pierre Vidal-Naquet (1977), there exists "a good use of betrayal" (the title of his book dedicated to Josephus Flavius, the author of the history of the wars of the Jews).

The betrayal of birth is truly a fundamental event: becoming aware of it on the personal plane means appropriating codes—latent contents—that could also help us understand the significance of events in our adult lives. However, it would be impossible to speak of real, experienced betrayal without first identifying and personalizing the two roles, the two protagonists, of betrayal. The logical question then would be: who is the betrayer and who the betrayed?

Strange as it may seem, the ways of betrayer and betrayed turn out always to be the same, as though they were interchangeable. The betrayed deserves to be betrayed and the betrayer cannot avoid betraying.

From the time of the first mother-child encounter, the mother spies, searching for evidence of a crime, suspecting the traitor in the child, who in turn will see the mother as the one who betrayed her. Obviously, although not verifiable, these experiences are powerfully present. Analogously, when the child becomes an adult and is overwhelmed by life's vortex, it will be silence which makes her aware that she is witnessing betrayal. Words or actions will at that point not be necessary to the understanding that something is occurring in which traitor and betrayed are reliving a fundamental experience.

The mother who spies on her son is beset by anxiety, unable to see him, or conceive of him, if not through her own projections. That anxiety becomes persecutory: her son appears at the moment of birth as her enemy. We might consider why, at a certain point, a circumstance emerges that is so strange and different from the one provided by common vision, but not by psychological intuition.

In any case, that strangeness is only apparent. We know that every mother, as she attempts to understand what is happening to her, becomes aware of the fact that, together with the child she has borne, she has expelled also a part of herself, her own life, interrupting a symbiosis which supported and sustained her. That expulsion is transformed in the mother into an authentic narcissistic wound: she is in fact separated from that condition which made symbiosis possible. At that moment, the child becomes the enemy, a traitor. However, presented with such a psychological constellation, what can the child do, when she—we must not forget—feels in her turn betrayed? Unfortunately, not much—except, perhaps, to attempt to heal, or at least relieve some of the pain of the narcissistic wound her birth inflicted on her mother. These efforts include attempting to reinforce the mother's fantasies by incarnating the child she imagined.

In my opinion, this aspect of birth-related betrayal is of fundamental importance. That we are imagined even before birth will be confirmed by any mother. From the moment she learns that she is pregnant, the future mother begins intensely fantasizing about the child. And here, I do not mean the usual wondering about how the child will or will not be, so much as her attempt to construct and model within herself a space in her own image and likeness, in which the child's identity will slowly take shape.

The fact that we are imagined even before birth, that even before we discover who and what we are—by looking at ourselves from within or in a mirror—someone has already done it for us, is of extreme relevance. Our existence and our autonomy are conditioned because, even before we come into the world, we have already been invented; invented by parents who also were invented. Betrayal, therefore, is inexorably transmitted down through the generations.

It was in this context that Murray Bowen (one of the pioneers of family therapy) legitimately incorporated what he called the "process of family projection"—that is, the process "through which the problems of the parents are transmitted to their children"—into the broader concept of multigenerational emotional interdependence (Bowen 1966). In this context, Bowen (ibid.) observed that, in the relatively short space of 150 to 200 years, an individual can descend from 64 to 128 families, each of which has made its contribution. As all the myths, mystifications, memories, and opinions will inevitably be influenced by emotivity, it will be difficult enough to know the Self or the members of the family in the personal sense, in the present or the recent past. Only when events dating back one or two centuries are reconstructed does it become easier for us to overcome the influence of myth and become realists.

Bowen thus introduces the possibility of parallels with the concepts of karma and original sin. And it would be this area that Jung referred to when, in his introduction to F. G. Wickes' *The Inner World of Childhood* (Jung 1927), he wrote:

> What usually has the strongest psychic effect on the child is the life which the parents (and ancestors too, for we are dealing here with the age-old psychological phenomenon of original sin) have not lived.

In fact, according to Jung (ibid.):

> We ought rather to say that it is not so much the parents as their ancestors—the grandparents and great-grandparents—who are the true progenitors, and that these explain the individuality of the children far more than the immediate and, so to speak, accidental parents.

However, Jung specifies that this kind of family "karma" is not only related to the life which an individual has in some way chosen not to live, but also derives from a natural ethic which is predestined and as such transcends human understanding; an ethic expressed as a law of compensation. Family "karma" is therefore also the consequence of impersonal sin: sin that in a sense has never been committed, sin that despite everything affects all parents and children even before they enter the world. Jung wrote (ibid.):

Such things as proletarian inclinations in the scions of noble families, outbursts of criminality in the offspring of the respectable or over-virtuous, a paralysing or impassioned laziness in the children of successful business men, are not just bits of life that have been left deliberately unlived, but compensations wrought by fate, functions of a natural ethos which casts down the high and mighty and exalts the humble. Against this neither education nor psychotherapy is of any avail. The most they can do, if reasonably applied, is to encourage the child to fulfil the task imposed upon him by the natural ethos. The guilt of the parents is impersonal, and the child should pay for it no less impersonally.

These are searingly painful aspects, against which there seems to be no recourse.

Consider the confrontation of fathers and sons, so different in their sentiments and ideas of life: so much strength on one side and so much passivity on the other. Such confrontations are moments of absolute desperation because, no matter how deeply one delves, no matter how fervently one wishes to discover all the fault possible (and it is always found), nothing can have been so determinant as to justify radical and ruinous differences.

Jung speaks of destiny's law of compensation. However, I prefer the idea of the quest for differentiation and the preference, instead of a generally mediocre lifestyle, for one which, albeit delinquent, is essentially different. It would be difficult not to feel that the mere fact of living one's own life already constitutes an infraction of which we are accused by the other, in response to that person's own existential inadequacy. Although Jung attempts to provide an explanation of these phenomena with the concept of impersonal guilt, every destructive action by the son violates that presumed impersonal quality, causing the most extreme desperation. In these cases, even strong and powerful parents can experience the sensation of being helpless. During such conflict, the limits of life are revealed and everything appears preordained. However, betrayal can occur even in an impersonal condition, and it is probably once more that guiltless impersonal quality which is in some measure responsible for the fantasizing of certain parents about their future children.

The fact of having been imagined—even before birth—is experienced, more or less unconsciously, as violence, as having been robbed, deprived of something. The reason for this is that our individuality, our particular human quality or psychic physiognomy, can become truly our own only through our own efforts, never as a ready-made gift. The son is led to incarnate the desires, fantasies, and thoughts of the mother in a dynamic which is then repeated in every subsequent encounter with a woman and—in a certain sense—in his relationship with life itself. It is not unusual that our most authentic psychic dimension fails to be realized in real existence, while the substance of the other's fantasies take on more and more substance—our substance. This condition, which constitutes a psychic prison par excellence, is far more common than one would imagine, or admit. There is a wonderful phrase of Goethe's that contains all the irony of this interactive mechanism: "I love you. But that has nothing to do with you." Thus, Goethe places in question the foundations of our perception of those we declare to love, or of those who declare their love for us. In this context, in a chapter of his *The Incest Theme in Literature and Legend* (1912), Rank refers to Goethe's love for his sister. One of Goethe's letters explores his idea that woman is not an abstraction of manifest reality, but is innate or created within himself—God only knew how—and that his women were all better than those one might meet in reality.

Asking another human being to conform to our dreams—forcing her into a Pirandellian mold, compelling her to act out another's fantasy, to recite a part, to play according to someone else's rules—is in fact an intolerably cruel punishment. However, victims of this expropriation of identity are usually also accomplices, because incarnating the projections and fantasies of others is in fact very reassuring. In the same way, the mother (or whomever is in her place, as we have entered into a far broader discourse of individual identity), fears that which is fundamentally and deeply extraneous as potentially able to impose authentic confrontation. That is why, as the mother conceives of and brings up her infant, it is easier for her to think and fantasize using images familiar to her, which confirm her own identity and capacity to mold others.

Life as betrayal constitutes a key to understanding all phenomena making up the existence of an individual. It opens up other, richer horizons, helping us decipher friendship, incest, matrimony, family, the death that confronts us and the death we choose. Clearly, however, there must first be the betrayal of birth. The relationship between mother and child is a power relationship because its composition is essentially asymmetrical. The human race, differing from other animal species, is characterized by the absolute vulnerability of its newborn, which dies without immediate care from those around it. Therefore, the duration of dependence which, as we know, is comparatively longer than that of other species, necessarily constitutes the basis of all human neuroses. Our dependence at birth saddles us with a debt that we can go on repaying for the rest of our lives; hence, the necessity of an early awakening—in the sense of being born as adults and becoming conscious of this power relationship—and discovering our own way with effort and determination.

That the primary relationship is a relationship of power is a reality; however, it is also a good metaphor to aid our understanding of that betrayal which marks the entire trajectory of our existence. The shadow of betrayal looms over the origin of the individuality of every human being, and from the time of our prenatal existence, we have been aware of the fact that differentiating ourselves from our surrounding world is made difficult in every possible way.

The idea I should like to advance here—and as a psychologist I could not do otherwise—is that, despite the obstacles imposed, there exists within each one of us a tendency leading us toward an exclusive and unique individuality—the same individuality which the Gnostics described as a "flash" and which according to Meister Eckhart resides, in a fundamental and definitive way, in the soul. Although the road to individuality is not without its dangers (the choice alone exacts its price), Jung (1929–1957, 18) considered the development of the personality one of the most precious achievements. In my opinion, it is undoubtedly *the* most precious. According to Jung (in the wake also of his own understanding of Nietzsche), this achievement involves (ibid.):

> saying yea to oneself, of taking oneself as the most serious of tasks.

It is also the greatest work of art a person is capable of. For, although we may work and apply ourselves in many fields, the area in which we become truly great artists is that of attaining our own individuality, which requires gaining access to our deepest dimension. The art of becoming ourselves is not looked upon positively by the collective mind because, as the collective mind is intent on perpetuating uniformity, it will inevitably see diversity and differentiation as a threat. For this reason, we may experience from birth a strange sensation of being separate, of intruding, of not having the right to citizenship in reality.

In the course of our existence, as relationships multiply, that impression of not having the right to a space, our own space, can intensify progressively, inspiring the Kafkaesque feeling of not having our papers in order. And yet, it is just that awareness of alienation, our claiming our place in the sun, the knowledge of our own uniqueness and diversity, which opens the way to individuation.

The realization that something has been stolen from our identity is necessary, because this theft is the primary betrayal, the most arduous to confront and from which no one is spared. We must also realize that, combined with the awareness that something other than us was expected, is the shock of being rejected for what we actually are. This original denial is also the origin of a superstitious idea of our existence, according to which we feel particularly fortunate or unfortunate depending on the success our performance earns us in the external world.

Far more difficult is basing self-esteem on what we really are and feel. We must have the courage to accept the fact that, in the context of that superstition, there can be no solidarity if not in the form of myth. And, as relationships between people so often are based solely on confrontation and competitive performance, it is less a question of solidarity than an unconscious complicity to perpetuate a way of life which mortifies the unique individual quality of each human being. Just think of individuals who, although moved to tears by the effects of earthquakes occurring on the other side of the earth, are incapable of lending a hand to a neighbor. Anyone in open conflict with the prevailing code of conduct will inevitably be condemned by the average person. The reason for this is the danger implicit in shedding light on the insubstantial quality of the average individual, who lives only to embrace current values uncritically, without ever examining his own morality or conscience on the basis of his interior experience—that is, by listening to his inner voices.

While both ancient parable and modern psychoanalysis—which, although different, have certain parallels—inform us that becoming individuals is the scope of our existence, we must not assume that that means others possess what we lack—a common, fatal error. No, the exhortation to the individual is that she must become herself, not another. Only what one actually is, according to Jung, can be healthy. However, the price in solitude and exclusion of remaining true to our own individual quality is high. Dostoyevski, whose ideas could be considered precursors of psychoanalysis—as Breger (1989) rightly observed—intuited the painful consequences that any process of individuation involves. The pain of individuation is shown by the itinerary of solitude, isolation, neurosis, loss of meaning, alienation, guilt, and inadequacy his characters are made to follow before reaching that moment of illumination and reconciliation with life. Dostoyevski's characters also demonstrate that the creative elaboration of the betrayal of identity is not a foregone conclusion. Only some of those entering that unknown sphere come back, mysteriously, more alive, more capable of living, having benefited from the flash of illumination which invested them; only for some will the open wound of the knowledge of individuality and the extreme difficulty in attaining it have rendered them infinitely more human.

Hopes and speculations as to our existence abound before we are even born. We are pawned, dispossessed of our individual value, when parents—and, mind you, not only the mother—depend on the birth of their offspring to satisfy some need (for example, as proof of their capacity to procreate, in compensation for something lacking in their relationship, or—what is even worse—in the illusion that it will save their failing marriage). They may also delegate to that birth conquests and revenges of which they are personally incapable.

In short, an unresolved problem is projected onto the child, imprisoning him. But the effects of the wave of betrayal that washes over the child's existence do not, unfortunately, end

17

there. The child's own life becomes a source of irritation. This means that, from the moment of birth, only with great effort will we succeed in conquering a real space for ourselves.

The sensation of being excluded has its origin in this primary betrayal. Our task thus becomes finding, or inventing, our own space, which is neither within easy reach nor immediately discernible, but is something indefinable, abstract, fleeting. As we have a permanent, desperate need of solidity, definite projects, and familiar paths, we will inevitably choose some activity or value: a certain profession, matrimony, wealth, success. In this way, the space we seek appears to us deceptively as something real.

However, with a bit of experience, we begin to understand that the space we really need, the place where we can truly be ourselves, is elsewhere. That fundamental space—which is the treasure we referred to, in its various mythical versions, or the "realm of heaven" of the evangelist Luke—is found within each of us: the adventures and dramas of the Philosopher's Stone, the Holy Grail, the Golden Fleece, the Slaying of the Dragon, are not set in a theater of this world of visible things or external reality. However, we must beware of becoming trapped in the literal, the concrete images proposed by such myths. Taking things literally, in fact, is an excellent way to betray experience. As the apostle Paul claimed, the letter does indeed kill. Myths are actually the distillation, in images, of the body of human wisdom acquired over millennia—and in its light, humanity is ever on the march, in search of truth.

The condition of successfully undertaking dangerous enterprises vividly recalls other trials that we as individuals must confront at different and differentiated levels. Jason went in search of the Golden Fleece, and Parsifal and the Knights of the Round Table went on their quest for the Holy Grail. Similarly, each of us according to her own light, during her existence must enter into the decisive and inevitable search for an object. The successful outcome of that search is the necessary prelude to the conquest of interior space. This search is the only possible response to that tragic, fundamental event in our existence—the betrayal of birth.

Three

The Parable of the Son
Who Refused to Be Loved

Your children are not your children.
They are the sons and daughters of Life's longing for
itself.
They come through you but not from you,
And though they are with you yet they belong not to
you.
You may give them your love but not your thoughts,
For they have their own thought.
You may house their bodies but not their souls,
For their souls dwell in the house of tomorrow,
which you cannot visit, not even in your dreams.
　　　　　　　　—K. G. Gibran, *The Prophet*

A new life is added to the family, included where there are
other lives. And, although births are inevitably greeted with ex-
clamations of delight, there is another oppressive, obscure side
to that joy. Under the veil of conventional reality, the new addi-
tion to the family will be obliged to develop along well-
established, inflexible, and genetically predisposed lines;
whereas, psychologically, a certain freedom of individual development would have been expected, in the sense of the child's
being allowed to shape his own destiny.

In reality, however, such autonomy is not always possible. Although every individual will follow his own psychological path,
he will have initially come into the world as the dream of his
parents. Consequently, as the weakest and most dependent creature on earth, he will inevitably be placed in an existential and

psychological perspective created by his parents' conscious and unconscious expectations. We have all experienced the sensation of representing a promise for our parents. *Our* growth, conceived according to *their* vision, meant developing in the way *they* dreamed of, fantasized, and desired.

The "natural" destiny of the individual, therefore, is not only to develop in a genetically programmed direction, but also to realize, on the psychological and existential planes, a project which is not his own but the result of the aspirations of others. By virtue of their initial supremacy, the parents represent all light, all good, all power. Just consider how the child's condition of inferiority and feeling of powerlessness in his relation to the adult can be translated, on the religious plane, into the asymmetrical relationship between people and God: theistic religions have always conceived of one or more gods with absolute power over human lives. Similarly, the condition of the child is one of total vulnerability. Physically, the child is so small as to be materially incapable of acceding to things. If we identify for a moment with the child we once were, we rediscover that sense of being powerless and the fascination evoked by the stature of the "big people," their magic ability to provide us with food, to care for us when we are ill, to repair our toys, and rescue us from nightmares. However, we also rediscover the sense of desolation and terror experienced when we felt abandoned or rejected by those absolutely indispensable beings, or their indifference, injustice—even violence, at times manifest and at others veiled.

The child in this context could be compared to a precarious, constantly threatened tool. And growth would appear possible only through the experience of that threat, that blackmail. Even the most clear-minded and responsible parents can at times be guilty of injustice, unwittingly wounding their children in their condition of total vulnerability and defenselessness—not to mention the real destruction that immature parents, crushed by a their own sense of inferiority, can unknowingly inflict on the child by using him as an object or an extension of themselves, a means of compensation. Consequently, human development is also the result of blackmail. Blackmailing parents exploit the unconditional adoration of their children: children will do anything to avoid losing their parents' approval, love, and protection; they will "forget" any injustice, any violence inflicted on them, if that would preserve the parents' good image. That good image is necessary to the child's very survival since, psychologically, without it she risks abandonment and death.

Often, the child's need to conserve an idealized image of the parents results in her repressing any negative feeling—very often justified—she has toward them. The indignation on having been humiliated, the resentment that follows having been ignored, misunderstood, made fun of, exploited, never listened to: all these familiar sentimental experiences are relived in adult life in particular emotional situations (for example, the willingness to do anything the loved one asks, to the exclusion of all objectivity as regards our own role, what is really necessary, or the space we should create for our own requirements).

This repression of feeling can reemerge dramatically in analysis and—just as not all parents are adequate to their role—not all analysts succeed in providing what is required of them professionally. In the latter case, some patients—like children involved in a very deep emotional relationship—experience great difficulty in identifying inadequacy in the analyst. In these cases, the infantile tendency to save the image of the parent is reactivated in all its diabolical force, the only difference being that the therapist has been substituted for the parent. The same can happen with partners, lovers, friends: considering this, we realize that what we are dealing with is just another facet of betrayal. We can be blackmailed above all because those around us unwittingly project onto us those aspects of themselves they are incapable of experiencing directly; parents project onto their children the Shadow they are incapable of recognizing in their own lives.

Parents who appear perfect in the social, worldly sense not infrequently will complain about an ill-starred son who is incomprehensibly self-destructive, violent, or idle. Generally speaking, behind this situation is usually a pathology affecting the entire family system. The son is forced by the parents to assume the burden of all the unintegrated Shadow aspects of their existence. A typical example of this is the apparently impeccable professional, whose Shadow cannot be identified, the frequent result

21

of which is that his diabolic dimension, the inseparable companion of his existence, acts like poison on those around him.

Jung (1929) commented on this not uncommon aspect:

> Nothing exerts a stronger psychic effect on the human environment, and especially upon children, than the life which the parents have not lived.

Once more in the context of the unlived life of parents, Jung explodes, or at least reduces to a human—all too human— measure, the myth according to which parents are obliged to sacrifice themselves for their children. During the final session of his seminar on Nietzsche's *Thus Spoke Zarathustra*, 1934–1939, Jung noted:

> When you neglect your own welfare in seeking the welfare of the children, you leave the children a bad inheritance, a very bad impression of the past.

In fact, what image can parents who torture themselves to the point of compromising their own well-being offer their children, if not the image of a tortured life?

By excessively considering our children's happiness, continued Jung, we commit a compound error because, paradoxically, as the parents fail to procure their own happiness, the children will not learn this difficult art. Such actions by parents generate the additional psychological error of postponing happiness, relegating it to a kind of patrimony reserved for the future. In this situation, the parents appear to believe that, although they are not happy, at least their children will be. What actually happens is the exact opposite. Those children, becoming parents in their turn, will repeat the same policy of postponement.

As Jung said, what is important is reciprocal love, here and now; only if the parents are capable of loving here and now will their children learn to do the same, and further:

> If the parents can take care of themselves, the children will also. (Jung 1934–1939)

Instead of saying, as is frequently the case, "I'm doing it for the children," Jung continued, the parents should do it for themselves—search for their own happiness, sacrifice themselves for themselves, torture themselves for themselves—and do it here and now. Postponing happiness for the sake of their children's future means leaving undone something they did not have the courage to do for themselves; it also means leaving "less than nothing to the children, only a bad example" (ibid.). Thus, an unlived life, even in the name of sacrifice for the sake of the children, is equivalent to a real betrayal of the lives of those same children. Once more, as regards unlived lives, Jung (1925) wrote:

> Generally speaking, all the life which the parents could have lived, but of which they thwarted themselves for artificial motives, is passed on to the children in substitute form. That is to say, the children are driven unconsciously in a direction that is intended to compensate for everything that was left unfulfilled in the lives of their parents.

According to Jung, this collusion would explain how the children of exaggeratedly moral parents can turn out to be immoral (ibid.).

An unlived life—and not only on the part of the parents—will inevitably spread its poison. Jung, in *The Relation Between the Ego and the Unconscious* (1928), describes his encounter with one of those apparently impeccable individuals, whose Shadow dimension seems to elude identification. Initially, when confronted with the man's apparent faultlessness, Jung experienced a painful sense of inferiority and began sincerely to feel the need to become a better person. Then, with his characteristic irony, Jung describes how, a few days later, he was approached by the wife of that eminently worthy gentleman—at which point, the illusion of piety and perfection was destroyed forever. For, as it turned out, it was the wife who paid—and dearly so—in terms of serious neurosis, for the Shadow projections of her pious husband.

We can also speak of betrayal in endopsychic terms. An individual who represses in his unconscious the inferior aspects of his personality—the Shadow, in analytical terms—betrays the wholeness of his psychic experience, and lives divided, as though constantly menaced by an invisible internal enemy. Endopsychic betrayal can also work to the detriment of the best parts of the individual, his talents. Such self-betrayal occurs in those individuals who completely identify with their Shadow, in a helpless state of self-contempt and depression in which that splitting is expressed on the unconscious level by a "grand" personality that compensates for the deflation experienced on the conscious level. Both attitudes are expressed, in interpersonal relationships, as a reproposing of the splitting dynamic.

The first form of betrayal, which we could define as a splitting from the Shadow, emerges in the projections of the Shadow and the constant search for partners predisposed—because of aspects in their own personal histories—to incarnate those projections. One example of this is the case described above by Jung, in which the man's wife took on the role of invalid, assuming her husband's neuroses. Children are usually the predestined victims of this sacrifice since, in their state of total dependence and infantile weakness, they cannot avoid absorbing the Shadow projections of their parents.

And then there is the other endopsychic betrayal repeated in interpersonal relationships—perpetrated to the detriment of the individual's most positive potential—the analytical term for which is the *identification with the Shadow*. In fact, the person afflicted with this splitting tends to project all light onto the other, living in a state of unconditional adoration—which is also a serious alteration and distortion.

Without falling into the trap of excessive generalization, we might be justified in saying that the two types could also be very much in agreement, in the sense that they fit marvelously together in an ambiguous, tenacious complicity. An enormous effort is necessary to become liberated from situations of this type, because in them subtle mechanisms are activated, all of which are unconscious, and of which we become aware only later, through self-knowledge and introspection. For some, this awareness occurs through meditation, Buddhism, Zen, or yoga; for others, psychoanalysis, and for still others, Christian prayer or simply love relationships capable of offering new horizons, expanding and enriching consciousness. What we call self-awareness is possible not only through psychoanalysis. In this instance, the words of the gospel, to the effect that "the ways of the Lord are infinite," could be taken literally.

If our goal is finding truth—that interior truth which religion calls God and psychoanalysis calls the Self—there exist as many ways to achieving it as there are individuals, and everyone must succeed in exclusively discovering his own. It is also the "narrow passage"—to use Christian metaphor once more—or "the unfrequented path"—an expression we might keep constantly in mind as we proceed toward death. Wandering from the unique and irreplaceable path leading to individuality is an act of betrayal, the cowardly consigning of ourselves, uncritically, to the powers of the prevailing civilization, its standards and values.

Make no mistake: I am not proposing that the way to individuality is a sure-fire remedy, to put an end to all existential conflict. For what we are dealing with here is a mystery, the mystery of life, the nature of which is always ineffable and contradictory.

Life in itself, from the moment of birth, is betrayal. What is possible for us, through individuation, is to use this betrayal in order to grow, to recuperate ourselves in spite of it, accepting its outrage while maintaining faith. It is a challenge to bear up under the contradiction of existence. However, that contradiction is neither speculative and philosophical, nor exclusively intellectual; it is the banal commonplace of our own contradictory nature that makes it possible for us to love a friend and at the same time envy him, to despise our superiors and still desire their power.

According to Kierkegaard, philosophers put up enormous philosophical scaffolding only to find themselves, in the end, living in chicken coops. And he was right, because human life is full of pettiness and narrow-mindedness, fed by superficiality and banality. We must master this paradox if we are to take ourselves seriously. Betrayal is thinking of our human condition in terms of absolute liberty, absolute knowledge, and absolute control of life's flow, when actually we control nothing at all!

The alternate proposition to that betrayal is also being aware of that impotence. The real challenge is trusting in something larger at work within us, something larger than the ego, transcending the first person, something that, in calm opposition to the message of media commercials, unites us in substantial and natural equality. Once that challenge is accepted, betrayal in its myriad of form and nuance ceases to appear as simply bad luck.

Through growth and overcoming a series of obstacles, we realize that the greatest degree of authenticity is possible only if we avoid identifying with what others think of us. And what can others know of us? For the most part, we are pressed into a collective and limited role based on a cultural model—therefore, dated and anchored in a certain generation. Obviously, the cost is high in both energy and suffering when one seeks a more authentic confirmation, which can only be interior confirmation.

This struggle is made even more difficult by the fact that the lives of our parents, if they have failed to achieve a similar victory, are nourished by our dependence. How often do we see offspring, no longer young, still living at home, and in whom that conflict, that straining toward individuation which at a certain point becomes explosive and inexorable, has not even begun. Many young people live in a limbo of possibilities, like splendid boats rotting on the docks. Their universe is reduced to the family shipyard, to the small reassurances and compensations, the small and not-so-small psychological crimes, inherited from grandparents and ancestors, and ready to hand on down to future generations. They run aground and remain on the shoals of family existential and communicative codes, saturated by their prejudices and completely unaware of the immense and unexplored ocean spread out before them. Parents conserve their importance and established roles by keeping the psychic dimension of their children under their control—which is possible only if the son or daughter remains *that* son or daughter, ensuring their psychological survival with minimal conflict. How many of us are still sons or daughters in this sense, bound hand and foot by an invisible psychological incest?

The last pages of Rainer Maria Rilke's *Notebook of Malte* come to mind here (Rilke 1910). There, the poet insists on his own version of the parable of the Prodigal Son, in which the legend of he who would not be loved emerges. It is not easy to become completely immersed in that work because its beautifully poetic language expresses something which is, psychologically, absolutely revolutionary. For Rilke, the Prodigal Son is one forced to leave his father's home because he has realized that what is loved there, called by his name, expected for dinner, whose birthday is celebrated, *is not him*. The Prodigal Son refuses the love which is not *for him*, those gifts that are not *for him*. In this sense the parable becomes one of he who refuses to be loved.

Analogously, Kierkegaard, in his comment on the biblical parable of the Prodigal Son, states that fathers are not sufficiently magnanimous to either send their sons away or understand that they must go—adding that in this way there is no solution (Kierkegaard 1834-1855). Rilke splendidly narrates the vicissitudes of that youthful quest, the contact with nature, the expectation of the love of God, and finally, the return home. He does not describe the return of the Prodigal Son as an abandoning of the search, but as overcoming betrayal, as if he understood that the father's house, where we are disconfirmed in our most intimate being, is a manifestation of life itself, the betrayal conducted by life (Rilke 1910). Perhaps the Prodigal Son would then remain, because he had slowly begun to understand how that love, of which others aggressively boasted, was not concerned exclusively with him. He would smile condescendingly at their struggling so intently for so little. It was clear that they were not thinking of the one who had returned. In fact, what could they know of him? Loving him had become by then very difficult. He felt that if even one did, it would be a miracle. And, for the moment, he did not want even that one.

Thus did Rilke capture beautifully the betrayal of the son, the tragedy of being unloved, of not being comprehended by the "love" of the parent. And he also understood the most human and wisest response possible to this terrible ambiguity: departure and return, which in psychological terms is the differentiation of oneself from the unhealthy aspects of love and the subsequent forgiveness and pity for parents who "strive for so little." In other words, the parent capable of loving him becomes a figure who is internal, divine, the "one" of whom Rilke speaks, whose emergence is slow, very slow, truly a mystery.

Another reference to the parable of the Prodigal Son is the

De Profundis (1905, 179), Oscar Wilde's long letter to Lord Alfred Douglas, the youth he loved. In it Wilde observes that

> Christ, had he been asked, would have said—I feel quite certain about it—that the moment the prodigal son fell on his knees and wept, he made his having wasted his substance with harlots, his swineherding hungering for the husks they ate, beautiful and holy moments in his life.

Reflecting on his own experience, Wilde commented that it would be difficult for many to understand it, and that to do so it was perhaps necessary to end up in prison—in which case ending up in prison was perhaps worthwhile (ibid.). What is the meaning of Wilde's interpretation of this parable? Does he connect the Prodigal Son's recognizing the sacred quality of his own life to his repentance and return to the bosom of his family? Or else, could we or should we assume that that recognition occurs thanks to the experience of betrayal and—even more to the point—that the "sacred quality" of life corresponds to that experience and not to events successive to it? And, finally, how should we interpret the reconciliation of the Prodigal Son with his father, whom he once betrayed by abandoning him?

This biblical tale was reinterpreted by André Gide in one of his *Poems in Prose* (Bergonzi 1990) to the effect that the return of the Prodigal Son is the admission of failure; that he searched for independence in his travels throughout the world, but was incapable of bearing his defeat, the anxiety and frustration which is inseparable from liberty, and returned home "out of laziness." Incapable of bearing the "betrayal of the family," he preferred to betray himself.

Another point of view is provided by Kierkegaard, who sees the return of the Prodigal Son—at least here not in conflict with Rilke—as a "return to himself" (Kierkegaard, 1834–1855). Kierkegaard also commented that, in centering all our attention on the Prodigal Son, we practically forget the father. Now, for Kierkegaard, the father in that parable is "God in the Heavens" (ibid.). We should, therefore, deduce that the return of the Prodigal Son signifies his return to himself in the sense that the protagonist of the parable becomes his own father—father and mother. In the parable of the Prodigal Son, then, there would be a passage from father to Father; that is, a passage from the literal dimension to a symbolic one. Jung (1917-1943) observed, and this can be applied to the initial phases of that passage, that in some cases

> the real therapy only begins when the patient sees that it is no longer father and mother who are standing in his way, but himself—i.e., an unconscious part of his personality which carries on the role of father and mother.

The condition of the dependent son is not bound to chronological age; it is possible to be dependent even at seventy, long after the real parents have disappeared. The image of the parents can in fact persist on a psychic, introjected level; the power resulting from its being unconscious renders it particularly effective in conditioning conduct and conscious choices. A maternal figure, for example, which overwhelmingly and negatively inhabits our psyche, as an introjected parental image, can literally prevent us from living in the autonomous and creative way that is possible only after psychological separation from the mother.

Often, a man anachronistically attached to his mother will encounter serious difficulty in forming a satisfactory affective and sexual relationship with another woman. Impotence, homosexuality, exaggerated libertinage—all are symptoms of a disturbed relationship with the maternal figure. Analytical work then consists of becoming aware of these tyrannical and false internal images.

An individual's chronological birth does not coincide with her psychological birth. The acquisition of an existential style in harmony with and true to our own personality is the result of the long psychological work of differentiation. Jung said that neurotics are truly superior, because they found it unbearable to remain in overly limited existential situations without meaning. One of the functions of neurosis is actually halting the progress of an unsuitable destiny; it is an illness which acts as a sign of psychic conflict resulting from the collision of individual inclination with collective dictates.

Individuation is a difficult and painful process in which

growth is not the result of intellectual prowess. Innumerable victims have fallen prey to the illusion that psychological maturity is acquired through the accumulation of theoretical knowledge, or by means of some special training. The usual result of a similar surfeit of psychoanalytical discourse is that the person in question, instead of changing, only becomes more pedantic and presumptuous. Clever rationalization is also the mind's betrayal of the heart. It is only to be expected that one who considers himself absolutely enlightened and omniscient will go around with the air of a prophet. But life, which is infinitely more resourceful, will usually be very effective in bursting those inflated balloons. The origin of presumption is also betrayal. Being more conscious of our own emotivity would make it less necessary to search for and become entrenched behind rationalizations.

Even psychoanalysts, and far more often than might be generally believed, at times hide behind their persona of therapist, identifying with some particular school of thought, rejecting out of hand any novelty, either in themselves or in their patients. The Socratic wisdom of reasonable doubt is unknown to such individuals, whose saddest defects are their intellectual presumption and lack of awareness of the emotional aspect of their lives. Once more, we are referring to the difficulty of separating from parents and the betrayal which they more or less unconsciously inflict on their children, for the attitude of a psychoanalyst toward his school of thought can often be very similar to that of the child toward his family. The convenience of delegating all responsibility to a school and the theories of its founding fathers renders the analyst in his practice extremely sterile and inadequate to handle the extremely variable conditions the analytical relationship creates in both patient and therapist. This phenomenon can also be ascribed to that common—and infantile—tendency to continuously protect the image of the parents we mentioned previously, which, in the psychoanalytical family, is represented by the founding fathers. Therefore, it is clear that betrayal is also and above all necessary to the children, a betrayal of those instances no longer relevant which could prevent the development of individual style.

Finding inspiration in models perceived as positive and in tune with her own inclinations is important to each individual and in itself a worthy enterprise. Even Napoleon read biographies of famous men! Thus, a psychoanalyst can be inspired by Rogers, Jung, or Freud. Subsequently, however, he will have to find his own working method, his own unique and inimitable style. Failing to develop a style of our own is betraying our expressive potential. Even though, during infancy, this betrayal can be ascribed to parental figures, in the life of the adult it becomes self-betrayal. Growth occurs in conditions of inferiority, because we are victims of emotional and economic dependence. When we decide to leave home, we must come to terms with the sense of guilt and economic blackmail, always waiting in the wings in relationships between inevitably unequal forces.

As children, we find ourselves between two poles, or perhaps more precisely, between two fires: behind us crackles the bonfire of family values and preconceptions, and before us the faint light, the weak flame, of our life project, which, if tended, will gradually become stronger. Think of all the cases of children born into families in which professional futures have been predetermined for generations: business, medicine, law, or similar occupations. How much courage is necessary for such children to decide whether or not that is what they really want! And then, how much self-knowledge can an eighteen-year-old boy, just out of high school have, to help him rebel against a project he feels to be against his natural inclinations? In this case, psychic health would be the capacity to say no to the paradoxical reversal of the roles of past and future, refusing any project already completed by others. Metaphorically speaking, this could be considered a second severing of the umbilical cord, and the new laceration seen as considering the "security" of the past a mortal embrace. Therefore, the dilemma here is whether to betray the future (ourselves) or the past (our parents).

Betrayal is one of the most dramatic of all experiences because it involves separation. But then, life is nothing more than a long series of separations, as our existence will be constellated to the very end with emotional relationships with someone or something; there is no emotional tie over which the disturbing shadow of loss or separation will not eventually spread. Obviously, separation from someone or something in which we have made an emotional investment causes intense suffering.

And yet, we not only cannot, but must not, avoid that suffering. We must instead open ourselves to it and experience it thoroughly—a process Freud called working through mourning, which consists of knowing how to experience separation, allowing the time and space necessary to process it.

As a psychologist, I am convinced that the choice is always in a forward direction, that the challenge is accepted because it opens up new dimensions. Thus, we will never be asked why we have not become something other than what we are, although it is possible that later on in life we ourselves will pose the question as to what we have done with our lives. If our lives have been spent in protecting ourselves from the unexpected and from change, we will be incapable of providing a response, because—having never taken the road leading away from illusion and toward authentic life—we will lack the elements or point of reference necessary.

If, on the other hand, our energies have not been spent in a kind of interminable *surplace*—which is no less exhausting than having joined the race—we will find a response of which we need not be ashamed, whatever it is; a response that has nothing in it of regret for not having had another existence in reserve. Although we cannot know why we were brought into the world, we can be sure that it was not just to stand there gazing off into space.

Four

Apropos of Roles and Trust

Hearts were made to be broken.
—Oscar Wilde, *De Profundis*

Most probably, we will never be asked the question, "What have you done with your life?" It could, however, take form within us at moments of crisis: on those dramatic existential occasions we all experience sooner or later, when, our backs to the wall, we must provide a response to, or in any event face the question and the existential crisis that it has created. The process of growth exemplifies this, as it often involves situations of rupture, inevitable separations that deeply affect not only infancy or youth, but the entire human experience. In other words, as life is an advancing, a progressing from one goal to another, and as humans basically are teleological animals, any progress toward a more advanced phase of evolution will inevitably imply experiencing rupture.

However, if it is the collective world—the world of family, group, or community—that poses the question as to the meaning of our lives, then it will not be our truly authentic individuality which is challenged, but that stand-in for our personality which Jung called the persona, constructed in compliance with established values and rules. It is also according to cultural canons that we define the conditions and mold the possibility of relationships with others, in order to facilitate rapid and unambiguous identification of our social role. It is as though our growth, although initially possessed of infinite potential, had subsequently been sterilized and reduced to a formula, as a natural response to the collective need for reassurance.

Clearly, it is far simpler to identify the other by name, qualification, profession—any label, in fact—than it is to open ourselves, as Levinas would say, to that person's real nature, troubling mystery, personality, and essence. Just consider briefly the fear and disorientation we experience when we cannot fit someone into some familiar category. Our difficulty in that case would appear to lie in the fact that the individual in question, because he is not completely identified with his mask, offers us glimpses of a personality rich in nuances which frustrates any attempt at reduction to a formula or label.

When we bow to the collective demand, we sacrifice that absolutely individual nucleus which is the foundation of all authentic existence. In fact, if our real existence is based on something belonging only to us, then bending to social conventions is tantamount to personal abdication, sliding into the impersonal existence of alienation. Therefore, it is essential that we decide whether or not the collective imposition is legitimate or, in any case, whether we should comply with it. During our development, we are continually required to assume a role, to evolve in the preestablished direction, in harmony with collective criteria of respectability. The bait used, first by the family and subsequently by that macroscopic extension of the family—society—is massive psychological reassurance. This process, however, is one of total deception because it conceals the most painful of betrayals—the confiscation of real, individual identification. The attempt to comprehend the world and come to terms with it is a creative process that can only be the result of the distinctive and original effort of each individual.

Conversely, in the family circle there is a collusion of roles and, where there is collusion, authenticity is betrayed. That conspiracy assumes a wide variety of forms, creating the most tortuous, devious, and convoluted patterns of behavior. Eric Berne, the originator of transactional analysis, has called these complexes of collusion "games," bringing to mind the linguistic games of Wittgenstein. The games people play constitute a way of representing human reality. In them, rules and roles are strictly observed, repeated, reproduced, and even passed down from generation to generation, to the detriment of relational authenticity and at the cost of much suffering of both body and soul. Berne (1964) defines such games as follows:

> Descriptively it is a recurring set of transactions, often repetitious, superficially plausible, with a concealed motivation; or, more colloquially, a series of moves with a snare or "gimmick."

And (ibid.):

> Many games are played most intensely by disturbed people; generally speaking, the more disturbed they are, the harder they play.

If the sense of interpersonal relationships becomes lost in the labyrinth of games, and the individual's authenticity betrayed, it will be necessary for the individual in her turn to betray the games—to die to them. This will be difficult to the same degree that the games appear reassuring, ensuring as they do a safe distance between the player and her real problems. It is therefore a matter of breaking that vicious circle of betrayal, which is the family circle, by redefining roles and the rules of the game. And this is possible through betrayal; that is, ceasing to unthinkingly consign ourselves to compulsive obedience and secret plots.

A fairly common example of the secret plot that emerges in the couple relationship is oneiric parallelism. Jung repeatedly noted that this situation often occurs in parent-child relationships when children dream the problems of the parents. In a conference held in 1923, Jung (1923, 53) sustained that children's dreams often have more to do with their parents than with themselves. He also describes the case of a nine-year-old boy who dreamed his father's dreams; that is, the dreams the father should have had, mirroring his erotic and religious problems. In that case, as the father was unable to remember his dreams, Jung decided to analyze the father through the son's dreams, with the result that, ultimately, the father began to remember his own dreams and those of the son ceased (ibid.). The unresolved dreams of parents affect the physical and psychic health of their children because those children find themselves in a state of participation mystique (to use the syntagma of Lévy-Bruhl embraced by Jung) with the parents; that is, a state of primitive identity with the parents' unconscious. This causes the child to feel the conflicts and problems of the parents, suffering from them as if they were his own (Jung 1926). That identity can exist because of the low level of differentiation of the child's ego. According to Jung (1927-1931):

> The extraordinary infectiousness of emotional reactions then makes it certain that everybody in the vicinity will involuntarily be affected. The weaker ego-consciousness is, the less it matters who is affected, and the less the individual is able to guard against it.

The fact that it was the unconscious and not the conscious state of the parents which has the strongest and decisive influence on the child was considered by Jung to be an absolutely terrifying problem (ibid). However, a solution to the problem— or, as Hölderlin put it, something which rescues from the danger—must be found. As mythology amply illustrates, only he who has wounded can heal. Subsequently, becoming capable of basing our lives on the presupposition of sacred fidelity to our own real inclinations must have that "primary trust" as a basis, that original experience of nourishment, mirroring, and empathy which is the gift of a healthy mother to her child.

Violence to minors exists in many forms, unfortunately including (more often than one might think) physical violence. However, when primary trust has been betrayed, we are in the presence of a violence the effects of which are infinitely more subtle and overwhelming, because it operates on the psychological level. Only love without betrayal in that early and crucial phase of our existence will instill that primary trust which later functions as a sort of platform, foundation, or container and is subsequently permanently interiorized for the difficult process of becoming.

The trust created by an adequate primary relationship is essential to internal solidity and a unified rather than splintered perception of identity—in which case, the material comforts in the shadow of which we may have grown have only marginal importance. Psychological work in the Far East and in the Western world is based on the search for and reconstruction of that platform where it is lacking, thus aligning with the common expression: "I must get back my faith; I must be able to believe again."

However, it is also true that betrayal takes form exclusively in the fertile soil of trust. It was in this sense, at least partially, that Kierkegaard considered Judas' betrayal of Jesus. It is pointless, he wrote, to criticize Christ for "having chosen a man like Judas, inclined to larceny, as treasurer" (Kierkegaard, 1834-1855). He also comments that the most dangerous—but also the best—way to save a similar type is by offering him unconditional trust. Otherwise, there will be no way to save him.

The trust/betrayal dialectic, so central to Christian mythology, constitutes the very foundation—albeit a changing one—of all hope of human salvation. In other words, a soteriologic discourse would only be likely after a prelude in the state of suspension in the dangerous passage from trust to betrayal and back, resulting in the reacquisition of trust.

Neumann sustained that the capacity to conceive of the world as a harmonic whole depends on creating, in the child, the feeling of being accepted, of being in harmony with the world. It is a psychological condition, therefore, rather than a strictly intellectual one that guarantees our cognitive experience because only the supposition of an order in nature endows the very human activity of scientific inquiry with meaning.

The German Freudian psychoanalyst Erikson affirmed that a healthy relationship with the mother leads to the integration not only of basic trust, but also of "basic mistrust"; the capacity to tolerate frustration, the ability to take note of the mother's absence without being destroyed. Hope, which he recognizes as "the first and most indispensable virtue inherent to the living condition," also belongs to the maternal sphere and is a modulation of basic trust/mistrust. The presence or absence of this internal disposition therefore represents the real difference between human beings. When the mother is no longer physically present to protect the child's explorations, her introjected image will continue to perform the same function. However, there is one exception: this solid and compact platform has its weak point, where it can become exposed and rendered vulnerable—

the dimension of sentiment. If this were not so, forming any relationships with others would be impossible, because it is only through that opening that we can perceive and comprehend the emotional dimension of the other, giving life to new sentiment. This fluid area can become the fertile terrain of betrayal. And, although we may be as defenseless as we were as children, we must venture onto that terrain, even at the risk of suffering.

Rilke (1929) commented that we wished to exclude all anxiety, all suffering, all bitterness from our lives because we did not know yet what states were in progress inside us, that we pester with our questions as to the origin and destination of all things, when we know well enough that we are transient and that nothing is so desired as transformation. If some of those processes have the aspect of illness, we should consider that illness is the means by which the organism frees itself of what is extraneous, and so it is necessary to facilitate the explosion of that illness, because that is its progress.

Individuals who appear to us as arid, rigid, unapproachable, will usually have rejected that risk, but in rejecting it they have also deprived themselves of life's real wealth. Maturity coincides with abandoning defenses, and it is in that fluidity of sentiment that the truth of a person is measured. Remaining open to the challenge of emotional adventure is ultimately what keeps us young. By avoiding identification with any role, or wearing it as a defensive armor against existence, we remain exposed and open to that experience which is at times gratifying, at others frustrating. And so, living one's own life inevitably involves putting distance between us and the collective. I have used the word *distance* purposely, because the elaboration of our own individuality implies the experience of separation: betrayal then becomes a way of access to death. Only by experiencing thoroughly what in psychological terms is called "working through mourning" will our unmistakably human creative dimension emerge.

The inability to face the risk of failure and the pain it involves is a key to understanding, in the context of betrayal, the myth of Narcissus (Graves 1955, 287):

He came upon a spring, clear as silver, and never yet disturbed by cattle, birds, wild beasts, or even by branches dropping off the trees that shaded it; and as he cast himself down, exhausted, on the grassy verge to slake his thirst, he fell in love with his reflection. At first he tried to embrace and kiss the beautiful boy who confronted him, but presently recognized himself, and lay gazing enraptured into the pool, hour after hour. How could he endure both to possess and yet not to possess? Grief was destroying him, yet he rejoiced in his torments; knowing at least that his other self would remain true to him, whatever happened.

In Graves' narrative, Narcissus knows that he will never betray himself. But, in this case, what significance can that have? Narcissus' limitation here is his determination to avoid separation from his own image, consequently avoiding comparison with other images or—in the words of Emmanuel Levinas—other faces, other intentions, other "ethical presences" (Levinas 1971). Also according to Levinas (ibid.), the face is present in his refusal to be contained. In this sense, he could not be comprehended and therefore incorporated. Narcissus could neither be seen nor touched—since, in the visual or tactile, the identity of our ego conceals the otherness of the object contained.

If it is the nature or aspect of the other which challenges the ego—in what Levinas calls the "ethical relationship," and which we might redefine as the "psychological relationship"—we begin to understand that the problem of Narcissus lies in the impossibility to pass from the identity from which he refuses to separate, to otherness, or comparison as well as in the resulting threat of failure, or what Christian David calls the *effraction de sa coque narcissique* ("breaking of his narcissistic shell"). In fact, David (1971) sustains

> love always submits its object to violence, as it is experienced as a unity in dynamic equilibrium, all love presupposes a breaking of the narcissistic shell.

What exactly does that shell conceal? The hidden face of Narcissus or, according to Julia Kristeva (1987), depression.

That constant lingering precariously on the edge of failure, that restless nature of the lover, is nicely expressed in one of the "rules of love" (adopted later by Stendhal) from one of Western literature's seminal texts—Andrea Cappellano's (André le Chapelain) *De Amore* (which also influenced early poets such as Giacomo da Lentini, Guido Cavalcanti, and Cino da Pistoia). Virtually a compilation of a "love code," it contains thirty rules. In Rule 20, in fact, Cappellano (1980) states:

Amorosus semper est timorosus.

The one who loves is always timorous (Stendhal 1822) because that person risks experiencing failure and accepts the concept— going back to the opening quotation of this chapter—that "hearts are made to be broken." According to Lichtenberg, the experience of failure is a passage essential to psychological healing. In this context, change and failure appear to be closely correlated. As Lichtenberg (1983) states, the tendency toward change is a result of those massive or partial failures that precede success.

It is a different situation for Narcissus. The objective correlative of his impossible passage is made possible by the landscape against which he is mirrored, a landscape uncontaminated by the presence of flora or fauna, a shadowless landscape containing a silvery, transparent fountain. How then could Narcissus complete that passage without betraying himself—that is, without consigning his own image to comparison and possible inferiority? The famous maxim of the alchemists is apropos here:

In habentibus symbolum facilior est transitus.

Obviously, Narcissus cannot be counted among those possessing that symbol; he cannot, like them, facilitate that passage for himself. And so, the good use of betrayal in the first place has to do with the ability to betray oneself, which is part of the symbolic dimension.

Closing the circle opened by our discourse, we could say that underlying any "possession of the symbol"—an expression, obviously, to be taken *cum grano salis*—is the primary trust mentioned earlier in this chapter: that condition which makes possible another way to relate to betrayal. If the "betrayal of trust within the primary relationship inflicts a perpetually unhealed wound" (Carotenuto 1989), then, consequently

> what is particularly damaged by the precocity of the betrayal is above all the capacity to structure the confines of the Ego, the capacity to relate to another. (ibid.)

We can therefore better understand the drama of Narcissus as the drama of one who, too soon betrayed, was consequently incapable of betraying himself.

With Levinas, we might consider a different, if equivalent, interpretation of that drama. For example, in the situation of Narcissus, subjectivity does not take the form of vulnerability and consequently takes no form at all. Reinterpreting Rimbaud's famous phrase, "I am another," which in a sense heralds psychoanalysis, Levinas (1972) asks whether the meaning of Rimbaud's "I am another" is really only alteration, alienation, self-betrayal—alienation and subjection to that alienation. That phrase, responds Levinas, can be taken as a comment on subjectivity, a basic condition in the sense of an opening, or the "inability to close oneself in from the inside." However, that opening also has an infinity of possible meanings. The intentionality of consciousness, as conceived by Brentano (1874) in his *Psychology from an Empirical Standpoint* (briefly: all psychic phenomena inevitably refer to something else) according to Levinas, constitutes one of the channels of opening.

Another channel is vulnerability, the baring of the flesh exposed to wound and outrage (ibid.). Therefore, ego is vulnerability. Dimensions such as sincerity or candor are related to the discovery of our defenselessness, being at the mercy of the other. Levinas thus sustains (ibid.) that candor exposes, to the point of wounding. And that is a risk Narcissus is not willing to take, at the cost of failing to become the protagonist of his own existence. In fact, does that image not represent the promise of that relationship with the other which Narcissus negates at the moment he fails to recognize, as it were, the other image and the other in the image—and is that inability to reconcile himself with the other who originated the desire not equivalent to being estranged from himself? As the Argentine physician and psycho-analyst Luis Chiozza (1986, 195) wrote:

> The pathological form of narcissism conceals a deep betrayal of self-love.

Narcissus is incapable of betraying his own image because he is unable to separate himself from it. In other words, that separation would be unbearable for him.

We have already described separation in love as the most dramatic of human experiences. The tragic quality of emotion can lead us to the most extreme and shameful acts but, according to Jung, the most shameful acts make it possible for us to survive. Consciousness, in fact, evolves from conflict. Betrayal brings both, betrayer and betrayed, face to face with death. She who betrays has understood that it is necessary to resort to painful laceration to change a situation, for only thus are transformation and the quest for individual destiny possible.

Five

Inimici Hominis Domestici Eius

But Jesus said unto them, a prophet is not without honour, but in his own country, and among his own kin, and in his own house.

—Mark 6.4

The primary context in which betrayal is experienced is the family, for it is in that nucleus that the first love pact is sealed, a pact that menaces and at the same time makes possible individual psychological birth. Anthropological studies have excluded any *natural* basis for the family structure as we know it, as ethnological models are extremely varied and often contradictory. Consequently, in our attempt to shed light on the psychological dynamics upon which the family is based, we shall examine that institution exclusively as it exists in Western society.

As the original nucleus to which the individual belongs, the family immediately takes the form of an ambience separate from the external environment, assuming a protective function as regards other potential relationships. Therefore, the fundamental sense of belonging, which is the basis of the family community, implies the separateness and exclusion of others, who are seen as extraneous, different, regarded with suspicion and judged as potentially dangerous. In Jungian terms, the so-called collective is elected recipient of all projections of the Shadow of the family; all internal conflict is denied and projected externally, beyond the confines of the family unit. Affective situations outside this nucleus tend to be considered the ultimate threat to its integrity. This stance is not surprising because associated with the sentimental dimension and its vital force are authentic transformation and the most significant events in our lives—events and experiences that unfailingly cause power struggles, tending to free us from the unconditional authority of the family (which claims the right to absorb all our affective potential).

The probability of survival depends on opening up to the emotional dimension which, although possibly a source of suffering, can also be the source of authentic creativity; an emotional dimension comparable to a mobile nucleus, as opposed to that solid nucleus generally known as security, which instead blocks our life's potential. In fact, the work of the psychologist and—to an even greater extent—the psychoanalyst consists of making possible the patient's release from the family womb and that outward movement which is a direct consequence of his opening up to himself.

The totalitarian tendency of the family and the right it claims to forbid its members or subjects sentimental forays outside its confines is, paradoxically, contradicted by a very particular cultural phenomenon: the prohibition of incest. That taboo inexorably renders not only legitimate but necessary "exogamous" relationships—relationships in the world external to the family. Yet the family continues to consider this evasion with suspicion, as a threat to its integrity as a unit. Perhaps this approach exists because, although the actual act of incest was made taboo, it remains far less controlled on the psychic level. In other words, even in so-called civilized families, in which real sexual abuse of children is nonexistent, very subtle forms of psychic abuse are common, in which the incestuous element emerges so powerfully as to condition the sentimental and sexual lives of all the members of the family.

Fortunately, the fascination of incest does not usually prevent the creation outside the family of new emotional and sentimental ties. Therefore, when an adolescent encounters first love, the parents—who will react with varying degrees of generosity—usually recognize it as the beginning of that natural separation from the original affective matrix necessary to create new, external ties. We could say that, at this point in the family saga, parents must make the best of the situation. Should that natural separation fail to occur, what will result is a serious blocking of the individual's psychological evolution. And, although by now rare, cases of young people incapable of creating affective ties outside the family circle still exist—those who, for reasons that could generally be called neurotic, follow a self-imposed, unbearable, and pernicious emotional diet. In other words, an incapacity to abandon themselves to their emotions is the result of their incapacity to separate from the family. When this original tie is not in some way broken, the perception of relationships with the outside world takes on the aspect of persecutory fear. Others are seen, not as human beings with whom relationship is possible, but as extraneous. The family becomes a school for lost opportunities, developing virtuosity in the nonencounter.

As we have seen, the family tends naturally to oppose any experience of growth or differentiation that might represent the formation of a concept of reality in which the other becomes positive, necessary, or vital. However, the family tie is so strong that even the creation of new, external relationships cannot in itself guarantee liberation from old interactive habits. More often than not, we go in search of situations that will permit us to reproduce, on the psychic level, our role within the family circle. In this way, the choice of friends, partners, even analysts, is strongly conditioned on the unconscious level by family models. As a consequence, psychologically incestuous relationships can last a lifetime; the incapacity to "betray" these mother or father substitutes implies the inability to reject and escape the family maelstrom.

One example of this limitation is the daughter who has maintained a very ambiguous sentimental relationship with her father who, due to his own individual fragility, was unable to adequately assume a paternal role, investing his daughter with an unsuitable affective burden, as though she were his little lover. This type of paternal figure, although there may have been no real physical seduction, seduces the daughter psychologically by presenting himself in the extremely ambiguous— and by no means easily decipherable—guise of a man intimately bound to her and at the same time unattainable. As a grown woman, the daughter can remain psychologically imprisoned in the role assigned to her by her father and as a result forced to perpetuate that role with equally unattainable partners. The incestuous relationship continues, with all its ambiguous force intact, always on the basis of a fundamental dependence. In that relationship, of which betrayal is not only a possible consequence, but also the inevitable premise, the woman will desperately attempt to reconstruct with her partner the parent reference that was lacking. However, she will also often unconsciously choose the least suitable partner for that reconstruction. The psychoanalytical term for this perverse psychological mechanism is *repetition-compulsion* and, although inevitable even in normal lives, it can in certain cases assume pathological form causing considerable suffering.

We relive the betrayal of the parents with the partner, and the experience of that betrayal is one of emptiness, an abyss in which we precipitate vertiginously when the other deprives us of the props supporting our dependence. The emptiness, the sudden absence of a reference that was taken for granted, the identity crisis unleashed by the absence of the other, cruelly reveal the degree to which we delegated to the other the confirmation of our very existence. As Roland Barthes wrote in *A Lover's Discourse: Fragments* (1977, 38–39):

> Waiting is an enchantment: I have received *orders not to move.* Waiting for a telephone call is thereby woven out of tiny unavowable interdictions to *infinity* . . . For the anxiety of waiting, in its pure state, requires that I sit in a chair within reach of the telephone, doing nothing.

Our sense of wholeness—our very perception of ourselves as existing—is therefore bound to a specific presence, and every threat to deprive us of that presence calls up the specter of emptiness, of psychic and emotional death.

The emotional encounter is marvelous because it gives us the impression that we exist. In fact, the autonomy and independence of an individual can be measured by her capacity to experience absence. What is intended here is not isolation (for isolation also introduces a cover of emptiness), but the ability to appreciate not only the company and warmth of the other but solitude as well, recognizing in the latter an unavoidable aspect of human experience. Solitude in this sense becomes an emotional experience, the nuances of which can vary because nothing lodges permanently in our souls. There is total solitude, in peace, resignation, and silent benevolence toward oneself and others; flat, cold, and unpleasant solitude; and melancholically sweet, expectant solitude. What is important is knowing that we can survive solitude. In the absence of that certitude, betrayal lurks, and the betrayal of our own solitude is potentially extremely dangerous. As Rilke (1929) wrote, that form of sadness which seeks company to silence is dangerous and malign.

Thus, we search for a point outside ourselves to alleviate our sadness, to contain our solitude. Fear and anxiety prevail, and into that black hole disappears even the dignity of the other, whom we invoked to aid us in avoiding ourselves. There is nothing pathological in seeking encouragement in friendship and love. Searching for these things might even be considered a sign of good health. In any case, what we are concerned with here is something else: the total lack of an interior nucleus upon which to base existence and the endless compulsion to fill that inner emptiness with external points of reference, whether they be people, work, drugs, or any other form of addiction. Two types of betrayal subtend an addictive lifestyle: first, the betrayal of the weeping inside us that desperately attempts to attract our attention the way a neglected child might; second, the betrayal of others, those to whom we turn to be filled, in which case the human qualities of the other are less important than the possible gratification provided by his presence. Consequently, failing to heed our own sadness, we are unable to empathize with the sadness of the other. In this condition, what interests us is exclusively exploiting and being exploited, silencing sadness with noise. At the basis of this misunderstanding is the ambiguous and ineffable experience of relationships within the family, in which emotion is consigned to the unconscious judgment of all its members—the greatest misunderstanding being created by parents incapable of providing a healthy example of welcoming and loving the child.

The family's cohesion is guaranteed by its interiorization as a collection of relationships that will inevitably be a terrible encumbrance to any new encounter. The Gospel of Matthew (10.36) instructs us that *Inimici hominis domestici eius* ("And a man's foes shall be they of his own household."). Similarly, in the Gospel of Mark (6.4) we read:

> But Jesus said unto them, A prophet is not without honour, but in his own country, and among his own kin, and in his own house.

Otto Rank, in his *Der Mythus von der Geburt des Helden* (The Myth of the Birth of the Hero 1909), observed the following:

> The old saying that "A prophet is not without honor save in his own country and in his father's house" . . . There seems to be a certain necessity for the prophet to deny his parents; also, the well-known opera of Meyerbeer is based upon the avowal that the prophetic hero is allowed, in favor of his mission, to abandon and repudiate even his dearly beloved mother.

That statement finds ample confirmation in both the Old and the New Testaments. In Genesis (2.24), for example,

> Therefore shall a man leave his father and his mother, and shall cleave unto his wife: and they shall be one flesh.

And, in the Gospel of Luke (14.26), Jesus takes that concept to its extreme limits:

> If any man come to me, and hate not his father and mother, and wife, and children, and brethren, and sisters, yea, and his own life also, he cannot be my disciple.

Subsequently, considering the above, let us attempt to invert Rank's assumption and ask how parents betray their children. One reactive way is using them as scapegoats for conjugal conflict—and, in fact, it is only by protecting the family nucleus that the child wins a space for herself in the parents' relationship—or, should we say, nonrelationship. Forced to restore an equilibrium that has progressively deteriorated, she is expected to confer meaning and purpose on an otherwise senseless and unfeasible coexistence. The child, moving within extremely subtle and viscous psychological dynamics, catalyzes the conflict of the parents and becomes in some way the theater of action, the stage upon which their aggressiveness or indifference is played. The old promise of eternal love has not stood the test of time, for the simple reason that over time individuals change, and the two people confronting each other today only vaguely resemble the two who stipulated the initial pact. Thus, in a relationship that has become anachronistic, the child is snared into the mortal game of the sadistic limitation of freedom of the other. No one is exempt from this exploitation, as it is based on emotional blackmail and maintained through a continuous sabotage of any outwardly directed initiative. Nevertheless, that experience is a necessary one because, as mythology teaches us, acquiring individuality will inevitably have some aspects of redemption.

After having reciprocally negated their own futures, the parents set out to destroy the child's. At this point, the metaphor of the "child-prophet" returns—that is, an existence naturally projected forward. There is no doubt that the future is initially an interior, and subsequently an external, condition. It is in this sense that platitudes about the elderly having no future should be interpreted, since that assumption taken literally would be nothing short of a tautology. The conjugal tie is based on a sensation of incompleteness created in both partners, each of whom seemingly entrusts a part of themselves to the other. This deprivation has, in fact, often been described in terms of mutilation or amputation: the metaphorical expression "He took my heart" actually touches on a deep psychological truth. Generally, every couple (and in particular those whose relationship is based on real motives; that is, love rather than obligation or vows) continually experiences that lack, with the result that they literally need each other to go on existing.

It is usually the children who pay for a couple's loss of desire, and that sense of guilt we have all experienced can be traced back to that unnatural request to bear false witness, to act as guarantor to a fiction. Freeing themselves from this role is no easy task, because the children are silently trapped by the dynamics of the parents' unconscious tensions. An explicit counterposition would surely be preferable and less pathological; however, that alternative is the exception and not the rule. Alliances against an external enemy preserve the mask of the family, with the result that the hostile energies nurtured within become less intense. Paradoxically, there is a greater element of hate in more united families (as the saying goes, "even in the best of families"). Emotional vulnerability mentioned is substituted by rancor, as its presence would render the family pervious to new relationships.

The fragility of unions would seem to be inevitable because desire, over time, is subject to wear, becomes eroded, and is eventually irreversibly dispersed by inexorable entropy. We betray our existence when we insist on denying that an object no longer responds to our needs. Abandoning ourselves to our emotions therefore means accepting being discarded as something no longer of use; it means discovering indifference in the eyes of the other. The negation of this tragic aspect of existence is sustained by a whole series of social expedients that, through the legalization (or, vice versa, the stigmatizing) of alternative solutions, prevents the free circulation of desire. However, it is common knowledge that there is no more powerful detonator than constraint. From birth, this tragic and painful aspect of existence is part of our destiny. Initially, the child must win the parents' love, in legitimate self-defense, as it were, to avoid being destroyed by them, given their overwhelmingly superior strength. That child, as an adult, will in his turn be faced with the same challenge renewed.

However, we must be careful not to confuse form with substance. The formal aspect would be the maintenance of a relationship between two people whose emotional current may exist or be totally lacking, or even be perceived differently by each of the two. However, that particular aspect is not relevant here, for it pertains only if an emotional context is inserted in the relationship, rendering the partners reciprocally necessary. Concealed in that context is the most painful dimension of life; the true origin of passion that suffers, cries, and wounds. However, it is only in this extremely dangerous condition—maintained by reciprocal need—that we feel alive. Bloch (1975), considering the verses of Hölderlin, wrote that where there is danger, that which saves will be created, and that that is the best we can hope for. However—he continued—where that which saves exists, danger will also be created.

This love can be defined as the spasmodic need of the other, of being capable of giving only when that act is functional to need. When this desire is absent, tragedy will be imminent. That need and the resulting reciprocal transfusion of energy will function only if a vulnerable nucleus is conserved, one that is receptive to the other's giving and possessing a natural capacity to offer. Consequently, our vitality depends on the ability to accept loss and conquest, absence and presence. I have on occasion encountered individuals who feared this painful existential dynamic, that polarity which distinguishes those who enter the fray from those who prefer (or have been forced) to succumb. The person who renounces, gradually and imperceptibly, closes herself not only to love and shared emotions, but to life itself, with disastrous consequences for everyone around her.

The most common form of suffering observed in psychotherapy is inevitably related to the sentimental dimension in interpersonal relationships. In fact, transformation of the personality occurs in relationships. Consequently, if it is in the sphere of relationship that we suffer, then the work of the psychologist must inevitably focus on and operate within that same sphere. It is in the relationship that the deep meaning of the dynamics of transference and countertransference lie: relationship treats relationship. For, if the relationship is the space in which our wound was inflicted, it must also be the space in which we are healed. It is interesting that intellectual conflict does not usually cause suffering. Of course, the pursuit of professional goals can require great effort, causing strain, but only when the emotional dimension is involved does pain emerge. Consequently, if an analyst conserves a certain degree of sentimental vulnerability and does not protect himself from the conflict of involvement— consequently avoiding becoming fossilized in a particular school of thought—his patient's quest for comprehension will strike a chord in him. For, unless he has the courage of an Achilles or a Siegfried, the analyst will produce nothing but useless and forced responses—as all responses sought and found outside ourselves must inevitably be.

Six

Family Circle and Hermetic Circle

Here only the right guests meet. This is the Hermetic Circle.
— Miguel Serrano, *C. G. Jung and Hermann Hesse, A Record of Two Friendships*

The consolidation within the family circle of certain apparently inexplicable relational dynamics will often, in the psychological context, prove to be an absolutely logical consequence. The individual is unwittingly drawn into a game, the real scope of which she is unaware. Her reaction is usually defensive, attempting to find external pretexts to justify her involvement. Against her own interests, she projects the reasons for her discomfort onto absolutely extrinsic events. And, although the real origins of that discomfort are actually very different, the revelation of this would result in her having to place in question those affective references which up to that point she took for granted. Here again, the prevailing mechanism will be the one by means of which the child desperately attempts to conserve the parental image. But in this instance, the situation is a desperate one, because the confidants are in the enemy camp. By betraying the family authority she could save herself, while remaining faithful to that authority at all costs means renouncing the discovery of a meaning for her own existence. In neither case will she avoid experiencing a deep, unconscious sense of guilt, and if she opts for betrayal of family authority, she will also experience painful solitude.

Obviously, by constructive betrayal of family authority we do not mean the mere betrayal of educational or moral values, robbing banks, taking drugs, or other delinquent behavior. Those violent syndromes can often be indications of serious disturbance in the relationship with the family; the child who has failed to free himself from the chaos and estrangement of the original environment attempts to attract attention and solicit care with outrageous behavior. In this case, it is not the parent he betrays, but his own potential for a satisfactory and creative existential evolution.

Also included in the context of positive betrayal is courageously submitting to criticism and scrutiny not only the values passed down by the parents, but the consistency with which that was done, as well as their subjective validity. Positive betrayal of the family means attempting to base conduct on what is felt to be right, regardless of the possibility of a clash with parents. And, if this is what an alternative option implies, we can well understand the family's strenuous opposition to its members experiencing their own solitude in the world, constructing within themselves a separate and secret place in which to move, to encounter others. Being alone and rediscovering ourselves in a private individual dimension without outside references inevitably implies a critical attitude and a tendency to analyze everything surrounding us. The prohibition against becoming concerned with our real selves is a direct result of the assumption that any investigation of the world must presuppose an investigation of what is, and has always been, closest to us. Moreover, whatever the response, experience can be considered valid only when it produces a resonance or deep echo within us.

In this context, it is not surprising that Adler considered the "problem of distance" of prime importance in interpreting the attitude of the "neurotic" (Adler 1920). The neurotic, from the perspective of individual psychology, is constantly concerned with maintaining a distance between herself and her problems, between herself and the decisions to be made or the action to be taken. That distance takes the form of symptoms, such as bodily discomfort and the denial of emotions. The rituals of obsessive individuals, according to Adler, can be seen as their interposing distance between themselves and their own affectivity. A phenomenology of distance and a phenomenology of betrayal are implied in that distance.

For example, in the previous chapter we saw how the family creates distance between itself and the outside world, as well as distance between its various members. A physical distance of safety—we might even say, a social distance—is included in the various established social conventions observed in various ways in everyday life. Adler speaks of the different degrees of intensity with which those suffering from illness express their "separation from the world and from reality" (ibid.), and he divides that distance into the following four categories: (1) regressive movement (a vast range that includes suicide and agoraphobia, anxiety and mental anorexia, amnesia and drug addiction), (2) arrest (which includes those "protective attitudes" such as insomnia and impotence, which "prevent the subject from going too far"), (3) obsessive doubts and "confusion of ideas or actions" (and here he also includes overemphasizing difficulties, morbid pedantry, retracing steps, or arriving late), and (4) creating obstacles (ibid.). In this context, Adler observes that the life of the neurotic, given his suffocated reaction to society, unfolds above all within the family circle. Afflictions in the great social circle can usually be traced back to the family circle.

Creating distance will be reinforced in many ways precisely because it is reassuring. Conversely, forming a relationship to ourselves will be perceived by others as being extremely dangerous—as though an interior life were prohibited. In fact, by retiring from the world, we reduce the intensity and redefine the quality of the effects the actions of others have on us. As our discomfort, as well as our well-being, acquires a new center of gravity, we cease being just another extension of the psyches of those closest to us, becoming capable of deciding whether to respond to or reject requests, recognizing their true form and rediscovering their deeper sense. This rediscovery makes it possible for us to reconsider our own discomfort, because we will have reduced conflicts and projections extraneous to it. A more realistic view of our dependence on others automatically diminishes the power of that dependence, permitting us to avoid much blackmailing and exploitation. Asymmetry or dominance in interpersonal relationships in fact depends on the degree of need, and when this is reduced, the power of the other will obviously also be reduced. The seeds of rebellion thus spring from the interior life. That rebellion can be considered authentic because of the dramatic aspect of any attempt at differentiation from the family. As Freud wrote in *Family Romance* (1908):

> The liberation of an individual, as he grows up, from the authority of his parents is one of the most necessary though one of the most painful results brought about by the course of his development. It is quite essential that that liberation should occur and it may be presumed that it has been to some extent achieved by everyone who has reached a normal state. Indeed, the whole progress of society rests upon the opposition between successive generations. On the other hand, there is a class of neurotics whose condition is recognizably determined by their having failed in this task.

The essence of our lives has less to do with naturally or automatically acquired characteristics than our potential to evolve: a personal process which is difficult and which can only originate in our most intimate being, that stronghold which is our quality as individuals. Having a particular family—any family, parents, sisters, or brothers, for that matter—should not under any circumstances be considered a condition inalterable or insuperable by our psychic life.

But let us set aside emotional aspects for a moment to consider the insignificance of biological aspects compared with the enormous importance of culture as an extension of the biological organism—to borrow a typically anthropological expression. The capacity to manipulate the natural element, acting on it and modifying it, is a specifically human quality, one which distinguishes us from all other living creatures. In the same perspective, our being born into the world is conditioned by a redemption possible only through the breaking of the unconditional pact stipulated with the family, after which, assuming the burden of guilt, we start down the difficult road leading to somewhere other than where we were intended to go.

Considering this premise, an analytical relationship should provide a new space, separate from the family one, in which the specific quality of the individual is not assimilated to something preexistent, but takes form and finds confirmation in experiencing—unfortunately, often for the first time—respect for individuality. The individual's rhythm is sacred and never violated in analysis, where conformation to the anonymity of the collective rhythm is not required. Instead, that rhythm is recognized as a component of personality, an aspect of a particular style and, in itself, valid. This is also and above all true as regards the common experience of betrayal. In fact, one of the bases of psychoanalysis, and one I consider particularly significant, could be summed up as the absence of betrayal. Betrayal is completely transvaluated in that relationship, thanks to circumstances existing in the analytical relationship, in which

> betrayal is no longer abandonment, the consignment of the other to a meaningless vacuum or extreme rejection—since the presence of the therapist is not subtracted—but the accepting of the prospect of failure and human ambivalence. The therapist relates to the patient with his entire being, revealing to him those aspects in which authenticity, respect, acceptance, prevail over any change of attitude. In this sense, we can speak of a substantial "absence of betrayal" which confers the new parameters with which to interpret the world, the new model of comportment. (Carotenuto 1989)

Parents will usually set their children the abnormal task of succeeding where they have failed. This is not just a familiar cliché, for the ambition of parents is in fact often without limits. The child is expected to redeem the parents socially and to acquire power: in other words, achieve something absolutely extrinsic to herself, attaining a goal she never conceived of or desired. Psychologically, the parents' projections can radically—even permanently—leave their mark on the child, and the effects of what Jung calls the "artificial unconscious" can be lethal in the child's future choice of a partner.

A good example of how the family circle inevitably and coercively models the life of a child is the situation in which the mother "keeps herself unconscious so as not to upset the pretence of a satisfactory marriage. Unconsciously she will bind her son to her, more or less as a substitute for a husband" (Jung 1925). Furthermore, in these cases, (ibid.)

the son, if not forced directly into homosexuality, is compelled to modify his choice in a way that is contrary to his true nature. He may, for instance, marry a girl who is obviously inferior to his mother and therefore unable to compete with her; or he will fall for a woman of tyrannical and overbearing disposition, who may perhaps succeed in tearing him away from his mother.

Liberating himself from family constrictions and asserting his own autonomy will earn the young person difficulty, pain, anxiety, and confrontation with persecutory images of the child fantasized by the parents.

In any case, the position taken by Jesus—the classic figure of a person betrayed in our culture—would appear a decisive one in the context of family collusion. The following message of Jesus is clearly one of division and conflict which, in any case, could be identified with potential betrayal (Matthew, 10.34-35):

> Think not that I am come to send peace on earth: I came not to send peace, but a sword. For I am come to set a man at variance against his father, and the daughter against her mother, and the daughter in law against her mother in law.

We have said that when a young person opts for autonomy, the struggle *for* something becomes the struggle *against* something; it is interesting to note here how the evangelical term *separate* has been translated by Luther into *rise up against*.

Objecting to this and analogous interpretations (which are not without their own inner legitimacy) is the German Jungian psychoanalyst, Hanna Wolff. In a careful psychoanalytical examination of the figure of Christ (1975), she poses the question as to whether or not the meaning of the above biblical passage has really been understood. Theologians may not have understood it; in any case, they do not appear to have provided an adequate response. We must consequently direct our attention—which could be dangerous—to the interpretative perspective of psychoanalysis. Wolff, responding to the above passage from the Gospel of Matthew wrote:

> Although this might sound presumptuous, only psychoanalysis can understand its profound meaning. In fact, Jesus "freed from,"

"divided from," the family collective, dissolves the ingenuous *participation mystique*, allowing the emergence of single, independent and responsible individuals. (1975)

Wolff would thus consider Jesus to be the first therapist, in the sense that the indispensable task he set himself was the struggle against the paternal/maternal bond, consuming and eliminating it once and for all (ibid.). I personally find enlightening the connection implicitly made in the gospels between so important a message and the dimension of the "betrayed" (constituted by Jesus as the bearer of that message); it is, briefly, that from one so betrayed, and only from one betrayed, can not only the suggestion, but the "commandment" to betray come clearly and strongly.

That commandment can be understood as the individual's need to assume responsibility for her own life, becoming father and mother to herself. Jesus would seem to have intended this when, to the multitude—that is, to the collective and nondifferentiated individual—who says to him (Mark 3.32)

Behold, thy mother and thy brethren without seek for thee.

he answers: "Who is my mother, or my brethren?" (Mark 3.33), and turning his gaze to those around him, he adds (Mark 3.34–35):

Behold my mother and my brethren! For whosoever shall do the will of God, the same is my brother, and my sister, and mother.

In a certain sense, however, the family nucleus nurtures no doubts as to its own substance. Although it may be bent by an external and more powerful system, its understanding of which might be slight or nonexistent, the family consolidates itself by prohibiting doubt. Consequently, any second thoughts or autonomous reflection are inevitably suffocated.

Actually, the individual's criticism of his own origins and the discovery of his own difference could be an important step in the direction of creating a family structure free of biological bonds, one justified exclusively by spiritual affinity. Hermann

Hesse spoke of a hermetic circle to which we all belong, which we can all consider affectionately and lovingly, because it was not imposed on us by the simple fact of our having been born into it. The hermetic circle is where "only the right guests arrive." Thus did Hermann Hesse describe that circle in his response to Miguel Serrano, who questioned his presence (Serrano 1966):

> "How is it that I am here?" I asked, uttering the words slowly and heavily. "How is it that I have come from so far away, and have had the luck to find myself here with you today?" Hesse remained still, bathed in the winter light, and then he spoke: "Nothing ever happens by chance," he said, "here only the right guests meet. This is the Hermetic Circle . . ."

What meaning can we attribute to the words of Hermann Hesse? How should we interpret that "Hermetic Circle"? And in what sense should we understand the phrase, "only the right guests enter"? We are not naturally destined to the hermetic circle; we must choose it, just as we choose to love a person outside our clan.

A parallel could be found with the community of wise men as conceived by the Stoic philosophers. According to Cicero, they assumed that sages were friends of sages even without knowing each other. And he continued (Cicero, *De natura deorum*, I.44.121):

> Nothing in fact is more worthy of love than virtue: whosoever will have achieved it must we love.

Obviously, we must define here the term *wise* (or *wisdom*). What is intended here, in fact, is not the possession of intellectual knowledge. In the light of our discourse, the definition would be roughly the one provided by Seneca in one of his letters. In this context, the Roman Stoic observed that

> no one is capable of gratitude if not the wise, just as no one is capable of good actions, if not the wise . . . only the wise know how to love; only he is a friend . . . We can say that true loyalty is only possible in the wise.

The hermetic circle can also, at least in part, be compared to Adler's *Gemeinschaftsgefuhl*—that is, that "sense of community" which Adler—as Hillman (1983) wrote in *Healing Fiction*—"considered the only realistic scope of psychotherapy." However, it should not be taken literally to mean a specific community, one animated by specific and rigidly preordained goals, for example, political or religious ones (ibid.). Nor should the hermetic circle be confused with a magic circle. As regards his second category of distance, the category of arrest, Adler (1920) sustained that the impression which this state gives is that of a magic circle of sorts surrounding the ill, preventing them from maintaining contact with the reality of life, facing truth, confronting certain difficulties, examining their own values, or making decisions.

The hermetic c ircle is therefore not a magic circle but a circle of interpretation and comprehension, a space within which dialogue becomes possible. The hermetic circle could correspond more to a spiritual family and, for those of us who have opted to become orphans of the old form of family, the spiritual family becomes the new point of reference. It is important to understand that such a reference point it is not a matter of a place outside ourselves, but an intrinsic reference, an expression of our particular psychological structure.

Seven

Nostalgia Deflected

*First Adam was created from dust, then Eve was cre-
ated from Adam. Therefore, the expression "in our
image and likeness" must mean that man cannot come
into the world without woman, nor can woman without man.*

—Talmud

We will now take a closer look at those dynamics upon which
the couple relationship is usually based and maintained, in that
same harsh but realistic light that revealed the existence of betrayal even in those phases of our lives in which, apparently, we
were immune. The adult couple relationship has traditionally
been chosen as the theater for the drama of betrayal. And how
much drama, narrative, media, history itself, is concerned with
this theme? Here, we will see whether or not our particular key
of interpretation for this phenomenon can provide a different
angle of focus or reveal some new, unsuspected facet.

In psychological terms, the fundamental premise to the couple
relationship is an underlying expectation, an anticipation of
completeness, reconciliation, wholeness. One literary source
which refers back to that essential condition is the platonic version of the ancient myth of the androgyne in Plato's *Symposium*:

The sexes were not two as they are now, but originally three in
number; there was man, woman, and the union of the two, having a name corresponding to this double nature, which had once
a real existence, but is now lost, and the word "Androgynous" is
only preserved as a term of reproach. . . .

> Terrible was their might and strength, and the thoughts of their hearts were great, and they made an attack upon the gods . . .
>
> . . . Doubt reigned in the celestial councils. Should they kill them and annihilate the race with thunderbolts, as they had done the giants, then there would be an end of the sacrifices and worship which men offered to them; but, on the other hand, the gods could not suffer their insolence to be unrestrained. At last, after a good deal of reflection, Zeus discovered a way. He said: "Methinks I have a plan which will humble their pride and improve their manners; men shall continue to exist, but I will cut them in two and then they will be diminished in strength and increased in numbers . . .

Zeus' precautionary sundering of the original physical unity of the androgyne apparently transposes into the language of Greek mythology the initially Hebrew and subsequently Christian mythologem of the expulsion from Paradise. In both cases, allusion is made to an original unity lost as a result of human pride and arrogance, that dangerous existential dimension which the Greeks called hubris and which signifies the guilty transgression of limitations. The myth of the androgyne, which contains echoes also of the biblical mythologem of the creation of Eve from Adam's rib (Genesis 1.27, 2.21-22), expresses the idea that separation and loss are experienced on the level of sexual identity as the incessant need to reunite with the other, lost half.

And here, the desire for fusion emerges in all its dramatic urgency. That myth narrates how, in the beginning, Zeus physically divided the androgyne in such a way that his genitals were placed on the lower back part of his body, and thus making generation possible, not among human beings, "but in the earth" (Plato, *Symposium*):

> After the division, the two parts of man, each desiring his other half, came together, and throwing their arms about one another, entwined in mutual embraces, longing to grow into one, they were on the point of dying from hunger and self-neglect, because they did not like to do anything apart.

Moved to pity by their unfortunate condition, Zeus decided to allow them to procreate (ibid.):

and after the transposition the male generated in the female in order that by the mutual embraces of man and woman they might breed, and the race might continue . . . so ancient is the desire of one another which is implanted in us, reuniting our original nature, making one of two, and healing the state of man.

There are those who maintain—and I agree—that all relationship aspires to union and that that union is transformed into tenderness and sexual love when the two protagonists of the encounter are male and female. This attraction has very precise connotations; what our search gives form to is equivalent in psychological terms to a longing for the fusional condition experienced in the primary relationship. That ancient dream is rooted deeply in our past. We are all able to identify with the fable of Prince Charming, that omnipotent figure of redemption able to put an end to our anxieties and fear of separation. And we may remain, perhaps forever, in the expectation of that encounter. The unconscious aspiration to return to the original symbiotic state is what is called regression to the nondifferentiated condition, experienced inside the mother's body during and immediately following the gestation period. That nondifferentiation, or condition of fusion, is comparable to a kind of paradisaical situation in which no gap exists between need and the satisfaction of that need, in which mother and child coexist in an apparently indissoluble narcissistic unit. Happiness thus conceived and therefore nostalgia projected into the future, is as such not realistically attainable.

In the interests of psychological equilibrium, it would be dangerous to give full credit to the illusion of possessing the ability to fuse with another, for that would be a distortion of reality. And, if fusion is our model of happiness, we will inevitably be disappointed. Our expectations will be frustrated, our hopes unconfirmed by fact, and consequently, our attempts at fusion will be doomed to failure. The predictable successive step in this parable of sentiment is electing the other as the guilty party. That process allows us to attribute *our* failure to the inadequacy of the *other.*

Much difficulty is experienced by the individual (and this is regularly observed during analysis) in searching also inside herself for the reasons for which her hopes are not "crowned. If we were willing and able to admit the illusory character of some of our expectations, disappointment would be transformed into disillusionment, which is another experience entirely. Disillusionment, in the sense I intend here, leads to a diminishing of the fear of suffering and a proportionate increase in the capacity to rejoice, permitting us to abandon ourselves in a more confident way to the ups and downs of life—no longer seeing adversity as a curse, but as something mysterious and infinite which can neither go entirely according to our plans nor be completely controlled. Accepting the fact that things cannot always go the way we expect them to is the exact contrary of incessantly following the impervious and tortuous paths indicated to us by our illusions.

In interpersonal relationships, these two ways of relating to expectations—the first based on a sense of reality and the second on illusion—will considerably determine the form relationships take. In fact, when the relationship is inhibited and constantly obstructed by speculations as to how it should develop and how each partner should behave, it is no longer a real relationship with another human being. Instead, it is once more a confrontation with phantasms. Life with all its unpredictability is replaced by our private and petty representation of it. The partner is easy prey to the parable of this dream, and from pillar and impeccable idol he becomes the source of boredom and disappointment. The other becomes guilty of not haven given enough, but is that not asking the impossible? These mechanisms are deeply rooted in the earliest phases of our development, and for this reason will be difficult to reveal as long as we remain submerged and imprisoned in the dream of how things should be. Searching within ourselves will lead to the realization that there is no more extreme challenge to our illusions of a relationship than the obligation to pass from an imagined to a real object.

Desire is the propulsive force of our lives; it is energy, history in the making, which transforms and transmutes, empties and refills. Our lives are desire, dominated and saturated in the endless quest for happiness. Desire, according to Spinoza, is one's very essence. But, the more our human desire for wholeness takes the form of an external object, the less probability we will have of obtaining lasting satisfaction. For, nourished by the phantasm of symbiotic unity, desire is the urgent need to possess an object which, when finally conquered, inevitably loses all attraction. This phenomenon follows the basic laws of existence, those regulating sentiment and the source of all suffering. It is in sentiment, and not the intellect, that suffering takes root.

Apropos of marriage, a brilliant journalist once wrote: "The trouble is that we think we are marrying a fiancé', when what we marry is a husband" (and I might venture to comment that the proposition is eminently reversible). So, if we substitute for fiancé the perfectly analogous *future husband*, which—thanks to the connotations evoked by the word *future*, extends the field to include expectation, or the imaginary—we will observe that that play of words correctly reflects the disappointment or defeat referred to above.

In marriage, the phantasm disappears and the object takes form. The union reveals its more human and limited aspect; there is no detonator more powerful than constraint. Marriage, living with one person, is usually seen as a means rather than an end: one has not deeply comprehended the subjectivity of the other. In certain cases, as grotesque as they are frequent, there is no real curiosity about the other, who is considered interesting only to the extent that she is constructed. Once we have captured the object of our desire, we do not consider her real world, her subjective reality. What we are interested in is, for the most part, a performance conforming to our needs, expectations, and motivations. The other partner will simultaneously fall victim to the same misunderstanding, revealing herself as being equally incapable of understanding the subjectivity of the other because she is also trapped by schemes of conformity. It is interesting and paradoxical that the two human beings involved in an apparently reciprocal relationship actually scarcely touch as they travel along parallel tracks, destined perhaps never to converge. Agents and victims at the same time of a nonencounter, they become the artisans of deep psychological and emotional suffering.

Another collective hoax associated with marriage is the myth of sincerity. We assume it our duty to be explicit, as though intimacy implied unmediated expression of every interior aspect, be it thought, fantasy, weakness, *in nuce* emotions, or that boredom which is an inevitable part of life. In certain conditions, confrontation with the other can represent a bridge to our inner nature; however, this should not be confused with unthinking and spontaneous outbursts which can only be harmful. Once more, the idealization of love means de facto its betrayal. In this context, common sense is consequently swept aside, because respect, love, and moral concern for the other require distance. Negation of that distance means a lack of regard for subjectivity, and it is perhaps for this reason that the most lasting relationships are those in which separation is an accepted part. The desire to share everything with the other, including the most intimate and private aspects, is nothing more than the desire to return—in a repetition-compulsion—to the condition of original fusion of the mother-child relationship, in which there is no division between the two individuals, only a copresence of both their psychic contents. As we grow, we constantly and in an infantile way seek to recreate that kind of relationship which, should we succeed, would be more collusion than relationship. According to Karen Blixen (1981), the real friend or son or husband has not so much as a small angle of his soul that he can consider his own; he possesses nothing which has not been divided conscientiously with others, and for him a secret is not a pleasure of the soul, but a cause for a guilty conscience.

Thus separateness, our only protection, is seen as betrayal. But by whom, and of what?

The basis of marriage, at least in the West, is typically a psychological structure of reciprocal and symbiotic support. Neumann, in his study, "The Psychology of Feminine Development" (1953, 80), maintains that this symbiotic structure is the basis of the family and the patriarchal society, in that it guarantees security and partiality.

I believe that this entrusting, this mutual care by adults using methods belonging to earlier phases of psychic development, unquestionably supports the logic of an authoritarian state, and is at least as detrimental to the creative patrimony of its citizens. Therefore, although it involves very considerable risk, embarking on a project of mutual growth is undoubtedly a good investment.

66

Eight

The Union of Two Solitudes

In either hand the hastening Angel caught
Our lingering parents, and the eastern gate
Led them direct, and down the cliff as fast
To the subjected plain; Then disappeared.
They, looking back, all the eastern side beheld
Of Paradise, so late their happy seat,
Waved over by that flaming brand, The gate
With dreadful faces Thronged and fiery arms.
Some natural tears they dropped, but wiped them soon,
The world was all before them, where to choose
Their place of rest, and Providence their guide;
They, hand in hand, with wandering steps and slow,
Through Eden took their solitary way.

—Milton, *Paradise Lost*

What is the deep-rooted psychological dynamic underlying the symbiotic union of the couple?

We have identified that union as the backbone of Western culture, which is a culture oriented toward forming fusional model-based relationships. Jungian psychology provides a key to penetrating the psychological significance of that union. The psychic archetypes, which Jung called animus and anima, represent, respectively, the unconscious heterosexual aspects of the feminine and masculine psyche. And those aspects, precisely because they are unconscious, can be experienced only through the recognition of projections. In other words, a man becomes conscious of his anima by recognizing his projections on a real woman.

Creating a relationship with unconscious contents is extremely difficult, as it is not an intellectual process. It is, nevertheless, essential to taking a conscious interior attitude that will make possible choices which satisfy our most intimate and basic needs. The less an individual has evolved on the conscious level, the more her choice of a partner will be dictated by unconscious motives which, unknown to her, will determine the psychological and emotional attitude characterizing the encounter. In most cases, the external marriage is contracted in total ignorance of the interior marriage (between female and animus, and male and anima). This occurs because those unconscious contents were never integrated, consequently excluding any corresponding, progressive heightening of consciousness. In other words, the union is formed before we become aware of the projective dimension—which naturally will complicate, if not make impossible, the difficult process of learning to know ourselves and the other. Balzac's statement in *Physiologie du Mariage* (1829) that "matrimony is a science" was not entirely unfounded (Balzac 1968).

The domination of unconscious factors may allow the relationship to function to a certain extent. Many neurotic marriages go on working for years, precisely because the real presuppositions remain unconscious. And haven't we all at one time or another found ourselves wondering how two certain individuals—apparently totally incompatible—have managed to stay together? They will usually have managed to do so because their every effort is directed toward maintaining ambiguity and a complete lack of logical consistency. Personally, I tend not to second those "reasonable" compromises, which are sources of suffering passed down from one generation to another—a hidden and unexpressed suffering because, as it cannot be rendered conscious, it is experienced in the shadow of silence. The acquisition of increased awareness in a relationship can reveal the hidden motivations—at times extremely destructive—at the basis of the neurotic solidarity of some couples. Acquiring that awareness requires much time, work, and psychological honesty. The therapist who eventually accompanies us on that voyage into ourselves will have to muster up all the ability and seriousness he possesses. The art of therapy, in fact, requires the entire human being.

Jung maintained that the process of individuation acquires a determinant relevance in the second half of life, when the experiences of youth naturally begin to make a working through of psychic contents necessary. As we have seen, the intense experience of youthful passions, even if lived unconsciously, represents an essential and extraordinarily creative aspect of the affective life. In explaining how our search for the other inevitably conceals the longing for the original symbiosis, we observed that in relationships grief and regret are often felt for something which either is no longer or seems unattainable. Thus our unconsciousness constitutes the main cause of the tragic gap between desire and reality. Most individuals live unconscious lives, but who can say, ultimately, whether or not that is a good thing.

What is certain is that in many cases it would be dangerous to upset the individual's equilibrium, even one maintained at the price of exhausting neurotic defenses. A psychic condition similar to nondifferentiation, in which the female anima of the man and the masculine animus of the woman lie buried in the unconscious, is a characteristic phenomenon on the level of conscious identity. Here, in fact, the woman relates to her partner and males in general in an exclusively feminine role, while the man's attitude toward women is exclusively masculine. Sexual identity at this stage of psychic development is therefore of the all-or-nothing type.

What would appear to be more important, however, is the condition of total dependence on the partner maintaining the projective dynamic. There is no space here for the individual relationship because impact with the heterosexuality of the other always presupposes a relationship with one's own heterosexual components. We are less interested in the concrete aspect of the relationship, its public aspect or its action, than we are in the psychological relationship subtending it, for it is here that tragedies in the relationship form. By excluding our unconscious countersexual aspect, we fall under the sway of the other, becoming, as it were, psychologically possessed, at which point the other can do with us as she will. This situation can culminate in one of the partners resorting to murder to end a dependence experienced as destructive. Such extreme situations, in which one individual has the power of life or death over another, are created when one has entrusted, consigned, or delegated a part of his Self to the other. Thus, the wound inflicted or received will be mortal, because the betrayal is total.

This reciprocal subjugation, based on a complementary and indispensable distribution of roles, constitutes the foundation of the union in general and matrimony in particular. Thus one might assume that, concealed behind the social mask of matrimony, is a sadomasochistic structure, a psychological condition leading to reciprocal torment; a game of reversal of roles in which each becomes in turn victim and persecutor. Consequently, there should be nothing surprising in the fact that the vampire Dracula has for a century remained an emblematic figure of Western erotic imagination (in northern and eastern Europe—the Balkans first and foremost—this figure already existed at least two centuries before the publication in 1897 of Bram Stoker's famous tale). The vampire's love is more than merely the desire of a perverse creature to feed on the blood of others, satisfying the lust for power through oppression, for that kind of love also illustrates the irresistible seductiveness of those who offer themselves as victims. Dracula needs the blood of others to exist, and the resulting contamination is so great as to transform the innocent prey into a vampire as well. Leaving aside vampire love, the couple relationship made up of victim and aggressor is an example of complete symbiosis. That continuous "transfusion" of roles keeps alive countless relationships. In fact, more often than not, it is not so much love as sadomasochistic dependence which seals and preserves a union.

By virtue of a strange psychological need, emotional relationships could be defined as power relationships, and which of the two partners actually pulls the strings is less important than is generally thought, because domination is impossible without the consent of the other. The term *psychological blackmail* refers not only to the maneuvers utilized by the weaker of the two to bind the stronger to herself, but also to the fact that, by calling on the power of the other, the masochist avoids calling on her own, which would involve coming into contact with potentially dangerous Shadow zones of her psyche. In this way, she succeeds perfectly in maintaining a clean image of herself. A pact of eternal love obviously cannot be underwritten by reason, for a similar pact not only implies our accepting, but also *expecting*, to have our entire future mortgaged "until death do us part." So luminous does the present appear to us in that condition that, like a blinding light, it cancels out our field of vision. In those moments of intense passion, we experience—or better yet, believe we experience—eternity.

Matrimony is today still considered a point of arrival. If, instead, it were possible to conceive of and experience it as a point of departure, the relationship would have infinitely more chance of survival—above all in terms of the quality of that survival, because any relationship is a journey and as such cannot exclude evolution. As Jung (1925) wrote,

> the psychological link between husband and wife will also be essentially collective, and cannot be regarded as an individual relationship in the psychological sense. We can only speak of this when the nature of the unconscious motivations has been recognized and the original identity broken down. Seldom or never does a marriage develop into an individual relationship smoothly and without crises. There is no birth of consciousness without pain.

One Jungian psychologist even went so far as to comment that, once that knowledge is acquired, love is no longer possible. But we might also consider the possibility that it could be just the acquisition of that knowledge which makes love possible for the first time.

An authentic relationship does not exclude the dimension of pain. In an authentic relationship, the partners do not conceal from each other life's continuous changes, its constant oscillations, or the sense of precariousness that makes us feel fulfilled one day and empty the next, in harmony with the universe one moment and hostile and wounded the next. By refusing to consider suffering, we close ourselves off to at least half the experience of life. And when that repression becomes a joint enterprise, marriage becomes diabolically transformed into neurotic complicity. A marriage of souls is possible only as the union of two solitudes.

The Mexican poet and essayist, Octavio Paz, wrote in his *Labyrinth of Solitude* (1959) that love is one of the most obvious examples of that double-sided instinct which induces us to delve deeply into ourselves and, at the same time, to go beyond ourselves and realize ourselves in the other: death and re-creation, solitude and communion. Consequently, the individual is simultaneously self-contained and in search of communion. When he begins to feel himself, he will also feel the absence of the other and consequently solitude. The implication of this is that the basis of love is a dialectic of solitudes, a dialectic which can confound and disavow what Paz calls the "social lie." Love is, albeit unintentionally, antisocial because each time that it is realized it destroys matrimony, transforming it into what society does not want: the revelation of two solitudes which create in themselves a world which smashes the social lie, suppresses time and labor, and appears to be self-sufficient (ibid.).

Solitude, therefore, survives in order to create another. Confirming this are not only the founders of the various religions, but also the heroes and poets of mythology. Solitude and original sin are one—and that observation of Paz (ibid.) touches on one of the basic truths of our profession.

In youth, because of the lack of self-knowledge, it is much easier for us to project onto the other our own interior aspects and experience surreptitiously our self-love, which remains locked in a narcissistic circularity. However, there can be no psychological relationship between two individuals who have not reached a certain level of consciousness, nor can there be consciousness without differentiation from the other. The other can never really enter our lives if not through an opening created by consciousness and, vice versa, consciousness is possible only by testing from time to time the limits imposed by the other's irreducibility, to the point of head-on collision, if necessary. The mirror reflection offered by the relationship can constitute the propulsive aspect of matrimony, in the sense that it can be an aid to recognizing the projective element.

If marriage represents no more than a magic expedient for negating the experience of separation—that is, the reality of the radical difference making up our existence as individuals—it will never be the abode of psychological relationship. We were all violently expelled from a paradisaical original condition, and our lives are spent in the attempt to heal that wound. That healing will occur through the very deep passion which leads us to say "you belong to me," "I have you, I hold you," unknowingly using a language, which is in a sense the language of war, to communicate all the intensity of our desire. Although the first choice in love often fails because it is unconscious, it nevertheless constitutes an obligatory step on the road to heightened consciousness and sexual identity. And along that road, betrayal lies in wait. Marriage, which is usually based on the cultural exploitation of unconscious compulsion, should be based on the union of two solitudes, in which the perception of the other's diversity is not experienced as a rupture of the symbiosis, but as a challenge to our narcissism. That challenge must be accepted— that is, if we place a value on psychic wholeness.

In the couple relationship the destinies of man and woman are different, because of the characteristic psychological development achieved by the woman, which can be defined as a process of individuation of the feminine. The woman will in any case be faced with betrayal: either of her own psychological dimension or of her partner. As Neumann rightly said, once the woman withdraws the projection from the external figure of her companion and recognizes this masculine image as something internal, she has acquired autonomy from the real partner (Neumann 1953, 77).

Nevertheless, that psychological movement toward freedom— the withdrawal of the projection—poses other problems, as it will inevitably be seen by the partner as betrayal. He will bewail the fact that things have changed, without even considering the constructive possibilities inherent in the transformation undertaken by his partner. He will feel assaulted, invaded, or rejected by that transformation. Neumann's statement can also be taken to mean that the psychological dimension of betrayal belongs— in a fundamental, positive, and constructive way—to the feminine dimension. One example of this is Apuleius' *Metamorphoses* or *The Golden Ass*, in which, as I pointed out (Carotenuto 1990), adultery is eminently feminine:

In novels, it is always the woman who betrays and, in fact, adultery is feminine. When this word is pronounced, only with difficulty does one think of a man, and even from a clinical point of view it is more often than not true that adultery never constitutes the heart of the problem for a man, as it can for a woman (ibid.).

A possible explanation for the attribution of a "feminine" nature to betrayal is the fact that the duration of the primary relationship is longer for the female than for the male. In fact, that difference results in the woman possessing a greater relational capacity and, consequently, the capacity to transform life. This would also explain why betrayal has a less devastating effect on men (who generally experience the relationship in a more superficial way) than it does on women (ibid.).

Mythology and literature amply illustrate (obviously in the negative sense) the "treacherous" aspect of the feminine. Eve betrays, as does Pandora when she opens the proverbial box, and Helen is responsible for the death of those heroes of antiquity who for her sake declared war on Troy. Andrea Cappellano (André le Chapelain) writes in his *De Amore*, that oft-quoted medieval *summa erotica* (Cappellano 1980), that females are false, since what is in their hearts is different from what is on their tongues. Therefore, no man can be in such confidence with a woman, or be so truly loved by her, as to be privy to her true feelings. Thus, the woman confides in no friend, believing that she is deceived by everyone because she is always deceiving.

Also, according to another medieval author, Maftre Ermengau (compiler of a *Breviari d'Amor*), nothing pleases a woman more than doing something she has been forbidden to do (in Nelli and Lavaud 1966). Medieval moralists accuse the female sex of vanity, lying, and betrayal; the same old familiar concept of woman traditionally handed down to us—a vision with which we could in part concur, on the condition that it be reviewed in a positive key.

Nine

The Terrible Torture of Silence

My nerves are bad to-night. Yes, bad. Stay with me.
Speak to me. Why do you never speak? Speak.
What are you thinking of? What thinking? What?
I never know what you are thinking. Think.
                    —T. S. Eliot, *The Waste Land*

In our traditionally patriarchal society, characterized by competitiveness if not downright aggressiveness and dishonesty, the destinies of men and women in couple relationships are not the same. Psychological development—one essential component of which is the differentiation of sexual identity—has always been conditioned by cultural canons. Preestablished roles, preexistent to the individual, respect the hierarchical order in a submerged system of reciprocal dependency. One example of that hierarchical character is a common phenomenon all of us will have experienced to some extent; that is, certain female illnesses. These explode as a result of an unsatisfactory family life and can actually be considered as being to some extent psychosomatic, for the very good reason that women appear to be particularly sensitive to the psychological dynamics of the relationship. In this context, women should be concerned not so much with the physiological etiology of their state as its psychological (above all, relational) origins. Recent medical research has identified psychological and emotional disturbances in the couple as the origin of many types of somatization: for example, dermatological problems, migraine, digestive disorders, nausea, lack of appetite, and various other chronic psychosomatic symptoms. Nevertheless, both partners must claim their share of responsibility and "guilt" in the couple relationship, and both will pay the price. What is left then to be said of imposed fidelity and the taboo of betrayal?

We are expected to be faithful, but to what?

In a patriarchal society the proscriptions for women in this context are generally not applied to men. Considerable effort has traditionally been made to prevent unfaithfulness in women. We might pause at this point, however, and make an effort to clarify just what that danger consists of. It can happen that at a certain point in a woman's development the question of conjugal fidelity becomes transformed into the duty of her being true (faithful) to her own psychological development. Regardless, in most cases psychological growth will not be parallel to the external evolution of the couple relationship. The experience of betrayal therefore becomes an aspect of the interior search for new ways to be realized, and as such can constitute a step in the direction of recovering individual identity. At that point, the dissolution of the bond becomes essential. However, we must not assume that betrayal alone favors an acquisition of increased awareness; marriages are full of betrayals committed but not comprehended—in which case, there can be no transformation. We might even say that committing a betrayal, without examining its content of anxiety, without somehow being interrogated by it, is the best way of changing nothing; the actual dissolution of the "betrayed" bond in that case will no longer seem necessary.

If a discourse on conjugal fidelity is to assume psychological relevance, it must include the far more difficult theme of fidelity to oneself. Betrayal poses a dilemma only if we are sufficiently sensitive to realize that what is at play is our own authenticity. Thus, although some individuals are unable to go on sacrificing their true sentiments to an exterior situation which does not correspond to it, many more simply are unaware of this problem because their lives *are* only the exterior situation. Considering also the interior world, emotions, and sentiments, not to mention confronting the contents of the unconscious, requires a great deal of courage and generosity—and, possibly, a mysterious predisposition to the language of the spirit, the soul. The obligatory itinerary of this interior voyage implies pain and also neurosis which, according to Jung, is the manifestation of the impossibility of adapting to a situation that restricts the free expression of individual potential.

Returning to the discourse on the psychological evolution of women, the emotional and psychic discomfort caused by the process of transformation can plausibly be transformed in its turn into more or less pronounced physical malaise. By shifting onto the physical sphere the causes of her psychological suffering, the woman moves her deep conflicts away from consciousness. Many years were necessary before the extreme importance of psychosomatic studies was recognized, and much time still must pass before women are liberated from the prison of their bodies. In fact, in our culture, the body is considered an aspect of the feminine. Consequently, it is only logical that women, albeit unwittingly, should use their corporeity as a means of communication. But there will be other occasions to take up this discourse once more, since recounting the betrayal of the body is one way of recounting the history of Western cultural codes.

The infidelity of women can become an inevitable symptom: either the relationship of the couple is maintained through reciprocal—and pathological—necessity, or else the relationship will not last, because its basis is exclusively conventional. The couple held together by a pathological alliance, however, is not the exception; in any union, one partner will inevitably incarnate the illness of the other, and vice versa. With the failure of sentiment, survival becomes impossible. According to Freud, those who do not love fall ill. I believe that love has meaning only if it is passionate. However—leaving aside radical extremes—we do know that love is the most irreplaceable form of nutrition. Freud also believed that the sensation of being bound to the loved one enormously increases the sense of the ego, and that anyone fortunate enough to be continuously in this condition could consider herself in a permanent state of grace.

That diabolical interposition of pathologies upon which the relationship is based is also the basis of all forms of psychological abuse within the relationship. One dramatic example of this kind of relationship is provided by Dostoyevski's powerful psychological drama of a forty-year-old usurer and the girl of sixteen he marries. The sadomasochistic relationship that is formed culminates in the girl's suicide and the abysmal solitude of her torturer. The suicide, with which the story ends, can also be seen symbolically as physical survival after psychological and affective death. The usurer, in the power game played with his young wife, uses a deferred system of communication that consists primarily of silence. The abuse of the power conferred by the sexual role often takes similar forms of communicative obliqueness. Silence is one of the most powerful weapons one human being can use against another; obstinate silence, the false expression of persecution, is in fact an extraordinarily effective weapon, condemning the other to a state of constant emotional uncertainty.

One of the most depressive and troubling images of the couple relationship is that of two partners dining together in hostile silence. This clearly indicates an irreversible disintegration of the relationship, which, at that point, seems to exist in an indescribable internal vacuum. The scene usually involves a man sitting in silence, sadistically waiting for his companion's inevitable question, "What are you thinking?" "Nothing" is the usual response, or else he does not even bother to answer. And silence is always an expression of extreme severity. Another example is a father eloquently silencing his son with one withering glance. Silence is an expression of judgment far more mortifying than any verbal judgment, because it negates the relationship by eliminating any possibility of defense. And, since the relationship belongs to the feminine universe, it should come as no surprise that this method is one used against women. Silence, in the words of the psychoanalyst Christiane Olivier (1980), is "the usual destiny of women." Nevertheless, the desire and quest for relationship is innate in human beings. The female possesses a greater capacity for relationship than the male because, as Neumann sustained, her relationship with the mother lasts much longer than that of the male who, because he must develop a different sexual identity, withdraws sooner from that symbiosis.

In the couple dynamic the male's response is often inadequate, childish, and silly. Few men evolve and integrate their own feminine component, which Jung called the anima. And yet, this is an obligatory passage toward forming real relationships. In the psychological context, the male must become ever more female and the female ever more male. Silence within the couple is lethal; it cancels out the other, negates his very presence, pushing him slowly into a dimension of nonbeing, until he no longer exists. The suicide in Dostoevksi's tale can be compared to the disqualification and discrediting that is part of daily experience; progressive devaluation and final cancellation. Submitted to hostile silence, we begin doubting our own perception: do we still exist? We send out messages, advance requests—all of which are returned to us, in silence. Women are the usual victims of this pathological interaction because they tend more toward relationship than prevarication. This could in part explain the fact that more women seek psychological treatment than men. Women will attempt to escape the stillicide of non-communication. However, it would be a mistake in this context to overgeneralize. Men can also be victims of sadistic, accusing female silence.

The most encouraging ambience for working at restoring relationship, in which communication is both significant and emotionally adequate, is analysis. So-called analytical silence, when used effectively, can also have a strong communicative content. In many relationships, the implied message of stubborn silence—which is difficult to decipher—is rejection. Silence can also be a vehicle of aggressiveness in analysis; however, awareness of this decreases its destructive and paralyzing force. What makes the method of communication between Dostoyevski's two characters so dramatic is the impossibility of introducing discourse into the silence, since that would have the effect of derailing the interaction from that neurotic track which causes so much anxiety and suffocation. Words are the raw material of human communication, and any pathological alteration of its potential casts the interlocutors into a painful state of noncontact.

Other psychological disturbances may be expressed in another way; instead of silence, a form of overtalking is used, the result of which is the same lack of contact and significance. Silence, however, remains by far the more crushing and powerful weapon, for it implies condemnation without appeal, which can create a sense of guilt as tormenting as it is inexplicable and unfounded. Silence creates the impression of having been punished without knowing why. Think of the usual reaction to an unexpectedly hostile expression. Confronted with nonverbalized hostility, despite endless labyrinthine attempts to discover the cause, the other is cruelly deprived of the only element which would help, the only bridge of access to her interlocutor's motivation: contact. Silence can be extremely cruel; it can contain a strong sadistic component, despite the fact that the one using it appears to be the victim, thus reversing the roles through a conspicuously renunciatory and passive choice.

The usurer in Dostoyevski's tale considers himself the victim of others, and that confusion which nourishes his persecution complex was also one of the motivations for his taking up the vindictive and aggressive activity of usurer. On the other hand, it is in the spheres of work and love that an exorbitantly high price is paid for any omissions and distortions which compromise our authenticity. The usurer, besides plying a humiliating trade, has created an absolutely neurotic relationship with his wife. This very common arrangement works not only at the expense of the woman, despite the fact that it is she who will always pay most dearly—truly a usurer's price—for those perverse mechanisms; she is the one in danger of being emotionally and intellectually mutilated, if not actually annihilated or, in any case, having her self-esteem compromised.

The psychology of relationship deals with personality disturbance as an expression of a pathology of the entire interactive system around the mentally disturbed person. The principle underlying all research in this area is that in human interaction it is impossible *not* to communicate. Silence, therefore, is also a form of communication, a deferred communication of the same type as double messages, oblique communication, communication by negation, and so forth. These characteristically obscure and undecipherable messages leave the recipient in a state of uncertainty as to his own perceptions, which although possibly correct are continually invalidated by the ambiguity of these forms of communication. They make up the language typical of schizogenic parents who present their children with conflicts the interpretation of which is at times impossible.

All human beings sooner or later come up against the shock of ambivalence, the love-hate of the mother, the father, teachers, fiancés, and so forth. However, when that ambivalence becomes an everyday occurrence, a rebus constantly posed and imposed, a disturbance in the child's personality is structured which is not easily reversed. Confronted with this pathological communication, which—as we have seen, is an expression of a psychological flaw in the entire family system—mental illness is the right response in the sense that it is the only one possible. It is also interesting from the point of view of relational psychology, according to which illness in one component of the family or the group provides a very important anchor for the entire system. It is not uncommon, during family therapy, to meet with resistance on the part of the parents coinciding with the first signs of improvement in their schizophrenic child. As paradoxical as it may seem, the healing of the child implies a revision and reordering of the roles of all the other members of the family—which obviously could be considered threatening by the so-called healthy members.

In Jungian terms, we might say that disturbances in communication and relationship are structured also as a result of the projection of unconscious contents; the Shadow, in particular. When, within the family or a couple, one pole is forced into a negative role, and she accepts that role, what is in progress is the projection of the Shadow and the acceptance of that Shadow by the other. Very often, the suffering partner absorbs the other's Shadow, in the same way a "mad" child often is invested by the Shadow of the entire family. The common metaphor for this phenomenon is the "sacrificial goat"—which should not surprise us, as psychology does not deal with abstract or otherworldly matters, but the daily dynamics of human beings and their psyches. Also, in the case of the usurer and his victim, silence as a means of communication can be seen as an effect of the usurer's projection of the Shadow. He presents himself to his wife as an enigma because he intends in this way to protect a grandiose image of himself, fearing that any confidential, affirmative, or friendly communication might reveal his true nature, which is mean, petty, and wretched. That character admits that, to his wife's enthusiasm, he responded with silence, which was of course benevolent, ". . . but she soon understood that we were different and that I was an enigma. And that was what I wanted, to be an enigma."

The usurer obviously also used haughtiness and the severity of silence to repudiate his own weakness, which he preferred to project entirely onto his wife. But there are also feminine figures who seem born to receive the projections of men. In any case, the discourse becomes very complex at this point because compounding individual psychic dynamics is the weight of the cultural and social environment in which the individual lives. Obviously, in a society based on patriarchal values, the woman is encouraged to take on the role of passive container for male projections, for better or worse. As the usurer himself says, in his desperate and hallucinated interior monologue (ibid.): "And the woman who loves, oh, the woman who loves would justify the defects, even the crimes, of the one loved." The "victim" accepts the projection of the man's Shadow and, becoming his accomplice in a game of silence, is swept into an underground malaise. She is too weak and too wounded to respond in any other way to her husband's affront: she is without family or independent means. Her husband is her protector and, consequently, her jailer as well.

Although women have come a long way since the times of Dostoyevski, the changes which did occur were extremely slow to take conscious root. The anima-women, as Jung called women who live to incarnate the projections of men, are still fairly common, even if the way in which the phenomenon is manifested has changed. In any case, as Dostoyevski's sharp introspection demonstrates, men would do well to beware of the passive submissiveness of "little saints." And women should as well, because masquerading in that the passive role betrays the intrinsic potential of a woman's nature, and the price of that sacrifice will very soon be evident, as we have seen, in the forms of both psychic and psychosomatic disturbances.

The victim's role in sadomasochistic relationships is actually a very powerful one, just as the role of torturer conceals a terrible weakness. The masochist, in fact, betrays his own power and uses the other's in the illusion that in this way he will succeed in conserving an acceptable image of himself: the evil one is the other, and this justifies his continuing to hate the other. The seduction, however, is reciprocal.

The usurer's wife reacts to silence with silence—leading to the extreme consequence, which is suicide. At this point, the only guilty party is the usurer; he is sadist, assassin, Shadow. Thus, with a single, final gesture, the "victim" immobilizes her torturer, and exits.

Ten

Euphoria Versus Joy

—I know that you are unfaithful to me.
—How?
—You know.
—I don't know.
—But you are.
—How?
—In what you do and don't know you do.
—C. Michaelstaedter, *Dialogue Between*
Charles and Nadia

As we have seen, adultery is considered to belong to the realm of the feminine. Literature provides endless examples of this view, from the tale of Apuleius to nineteenth-century novels—most of which revolve around the character of an adulterous woman. *Madame Bovary* is only one eminent example. According to Tony Tanner (1979), adultery could be considered "generative of western literature, as we know it." And examples abound, from the time of Homer to the present. The literature of ancient Greece gave us Paris and Helen, whose transgression was disastrous for that heroic world, and Clytemnestra and Aegisthus. Medieval chivalrous literature gave us Lancelot and his Guinevere, whose transgression sounded the death knell for the knights of the Round Table, and the equally famous Tristan and Iseult. Tanner also cites late Shakespearean drama, the English Restoration, and, above all, nineteenth- and twentieth-century novels (Stendhal's *Rouge et Noir*, Tolstoi's *Anna Karenina*, and Lawrence's *Lady Chatterley's Lover*). Leopold Bloom, the protagonist of Joyce's *Ulysses*, another in the long line of men betrayed, wanders the streets of Dublin amid small crimes and misdemeanors, for the space of a day in his life; a day that is the sum total of every day and perhaps every life, played out to the rhythm of a wife's betrayal. Bataille's paradox (1962, 64):

> Sometimes an intangible taboo is violated . . .

has always been a part, and therefore the strength, of the world of the novel (ibid.).

Tanner, in her conclusion to a study on the theme of adultery in the novel, comments that without adultery (or at least without the perennial presence of its possibility), the novel would have been deprived of much of its narrative vitality. Certainly, without adultery, the history of the novel would be very different and also perhaps a good deal poorer. Adultery ultimately provides something to write about, access to a world charged with meaning. And, obviously, it is something that concerns the novel less than it does life itself. Thus, we might also say that life might also be considerably poorer without the painful access to the world of meaning provided by adultery. Let us now consider that crucial experience—betrayal—which occurs in the most natural, as well as the most obvious context: the couple relationship.

It is of little importance whether the affective tie was institutionalized or not; the essential psychological aspects of matrimony and cohabitation are the same, with the exception of a few subtle differences or complications characterizing each alternative. The inevitable lament after a betrayal is "Why did he (or she) do it?" And here one of life's most tragic, solitary, and painful experiences begins, with betrayed and betrayer face to face in the pathetic attempt to comprehend an event that no words can explain. For the partner betrayed, searching for that explanation is part of the process of working out mourning, in which that question does not find meaning in a response— always and inevitably unsatisfactory—but in the time taken to organize a possible defense. The person who has been betrayed is devastated, inexpressibly weakened before a truth only intuited, which is incomprehensible to her because it is buried at the most archaic and primitive psychic levels of unconsciousness.

The partner who has betrayed had been entrusted with the impossible task of healing the rupture experienced in the relationship with the parents. However, as the child did not possess the capacity, substance, or creativity to compensate for that loss of love, so the adult—in whom the wound received in the parent-child relationship was never healed—could not possibly hope to exorcise it once and for all through falling in love.

When we love, in the unconscious desire to eliminate the original wound, and are once more abandoned and consigned to the anxiety of loss, the only road to salvation is through the process of growth, evolution. Only thus will we realize how anachronistic the desire for total and nondifferentiated fusion is, and how that desire must inevitably be frustrated, since life itself is an unending succession of separation and differentiation.

In fact, the child has need of mirroring and containment by the mother, which is natural and indispensable to a healthy structuring of the ego. Unfortunately, the inadequacy of the maternal figure or the family environment often prevents that need from being satisfied. The result of this is that psychological maturity in the relational, sexual, and sentimental spheres will not be on a par either with the individual's chronological and intellectual development or sometimes even those important existential areas such as work and the creation of a family. This imbalance reflects the high percentage of men and women whose emotional and affective development has been blocked at the dawn of experience, in the first years of life.

Individual psychological birth is impossible without the experience of betrayal. People come into the world, entering a condition of ontological exposure to the mortification of betrayal: the betrayal of life by death, betrayal through hate, betrayal of the primary unity through birth itself. Without growth through the experience of betrayal, we remain anchored in the unconscious, repetitive quest for fusion with another and, consequently, never gain access to the mystery of life. In this way, we refuse to assume the burden and responsibility implied by our existence as unique and separate beings. The moment our infantile desire for plenitude is addressed to a concrete object, loss has already occurred. It has been my experience (Carotenuto 1987) that the existence within us of a helpless child ready to place himself unconditionally in the hands of the other is the very condition that exposes us to disappointment. However, it is also the humus of the love experience, the ecstatic fusion with the lover. There is, and can be, no maturity without a conscious rapport with our infantile dimension.

The reaction of one who has been abandoned is intense and visceral, and being aware that the sentiments in question considerably transcend the contingent affective tie does nothing to lessen the intensity of the suffering. Echoing ancient models of relationships that had ingenuously been relegated to the past, betrayal is, once more, an asymmetrical situation. The love pact has been broken and, simultaneously, the implicit guarantee of that reciprocal dependence which ensured its solidity has ceased to exist.

The autonomy demonstrated by the betrayer is doubly devastating because it obviously implies the creation of another dependence *outside* the rejected relationship. No one withdraws from a relationship without having already reinvested her energies elsewhere—whether she admits it or not. And that is enough to restore that internal balance which is always a fundamental aspect of the life of the couple. Of course, the players in this game are not fairly matched, for the betrayer—captured by a new love—has found a new equilibrium, without having been even momentarily thrown off balance by the upsetting of the old one.

The one betrayed, on the other hand, suddenly deprived of his center of gravity, has not only been mortified by an irreparable devaluation, but has also been exposed in an indescribably vulnerable state. The abandonment he demonstrated in approaching the lover has become unbearable nudity. Wounded in the deepest trust he placed in the other, so similar to the absolute dependence experienced in the primary relationship, the one betrayed feels consigned to death. The suspended temporality experienced in the passionate relationship has been interrupted by betrayal, and the eternal that lulled him has suddenly been transformed into a void. Trapped in an immobile present, there seems no way out. The intensity of that desperation is equal to the intensity of the exaltation experienced up until then—in both cases absolute and irrevocable.

The passion of love can reach an intensity rare in other passions, as it constitutes a narcissistically self-contained universe. Lovers live clandestine, secret lives, almost as if to protect themselves from the world's invidious attacks. That concept is nicely expressed in the conclusion of the second volume of Andrea Cappellano's *De Amore* (1980):

> Amore, dach'e' palesato, rade volte suole durare.
> [Love, once disclosed, rarely lasts.]

The collective perception of the couple is one of potential threat, challenge, and affront. The couple could constitute a conspiracy or criminal association because, forgetful of any ethical sense, it exists in a dimension beyond good and evil. In its autonomy it has no need of external confirmation and is possibly even nourished by the transgressive opposition to social norms. This experience offers such complete gratification as to exclude any possibility of compensation when it ceases.

As we have said, the end of a relationship is experienced as the sudden absence of meaning; the individual is plunged back into a daily routine as oppressive as her passion had been intense. The lover has become a stranger; his thoughts are elsewhere and no longer include us. We have been canceled, literally thrown out. The lie usually resorted to in such cases, and by both partners, represents for one an attempt to survive and for the other a way to alleviate a feeling of guilt. It is at that point that we are precipitated suddenly from a sense of eternity to the opposite condition of the most vulnerable precariousness, in which we will doubt that we still exist; in other words, a sensation of death. Instead of feeling, as we previously did, more alive than ever, we have become evanescent, immaterial phantasms. We no longer possess anything; the other has taken with him, dispossessed us of our soul's wealth and the beauty of our body (because the beauty of the body is above all the means with which every lover gives pleasure to the partner). But, previously, combined with our gratitude for the pleasure of the orgasm, there had also been an astonishment of sorts at the absence of any aggression, at those moments when we were so defenseless and vulnerable. These could be the images that emerge with such intensity, causing suspicion and the violent explosion of jealousy. All things considered, having asked everything of our partner, we are also convinced that we have *given* everything. We do not realize that it is precisely in that request and the absolute surrender of ourselves that the seed of imminent abandonment lies, one of the possible forms of which is betrayal. It is impossible, in fact, for anyone to support so intense an investment for long without feeling crushed.

In passionate love, the other's presence seems essential to the survival of our ego—which is illustrative of the fragile and dependent nature of its functioning. In fact, the indisputable strength which the ego can acquire in a passionate love affair can also be pervaded by an ineffable, nagging apprehension which could be considered the very lifeblood of dependence. The existence of the ego is reinforced by the existence of the other (to whom we are passionately bound). We have completely abdicated ourselves, and how dangerous this situation is becomes painfully clear when the other withdraws, leaving us in a state of defenselessness and deprivation. And yet, this painful experience offers an extraordinary opportunity for psychological growth, precisely due to its devastating force (driving the more vulnerable at times to suicide). Only by experiencing thoroughly that event will we acquire true self-awareness. If the couple relationship lasts, and the ego of each of the partners succeeds in maintaining a psychological relationship with the other, both individuals will undoubtedly have been strengthened.

If the analyst is sincere, when asked how she has survived years of continuous contact with suffering, she will not attribute that resistance to her long years of immunizing training (which is the usual response given by incompetents to other incompetents). The most legitimate explanation for her ability to maintain a creative relationship with her own suffering and the suffering of so many other human beings would be the affective balance she has acquired in her own private life. However, we must beware of falling into the trap of creating an idealized and larger-than-life figure of the psychoanalyst, for she is ultimately only human and therefore also capable of error. The real ability of a psychoanalyst lies her capacity to change course when she realizes that the progress of a therapy has taken an erroneous turn.

Consequently, as psychoanalysis deals with deeply involving emotional situations, the emotional and affective stability of the analyst is essential, because otherwise, she could end up seriously polluting the madness of her patients with her own "madness."

The inevitability of separation and the end of love's illusion does not mean that the solitary life is a more realistic or more courageous alternative; betrayal is part of the insuppressible dialectic of life itself. I personally believe that it takes more courage to maintain a relationship than to live alone, for the life of a couple is constantly exposed to the possibility of betrayal (the effects of which are physical as well as a psychic).

Although the reactions to betrayal are many, the most common one is the strategy of the Gordian knot. The young king of Phrygia, when confronted with the stubborn knot, had no alternative other than to promise Asia to the man who succeeded in solving the problem. Alexander the Great solved the problem, but only because he realized that the only real solution was a drastic one.

As we have said, in great loves, separation and betrayal are experienced as "mortal stabs"—to the body, as well as to the soul. Being abandoned by the loved one creates a series of physical symptoms, although we may not always be aware of the connection between them and our devastated psychic condition. Very often, emotional suffering that is suffocated and repressed at the conscious level can becomes real physical discomfort. Believing that the other has taken away a part of us, we feel mutilated; our bodily wholeness and harmony are destroyed—as if the betrayer, after having abandoned us, acquired an auxiliary ego: the ego stolen from us. In this way, the betrayer is seen by the betrayed in an obsessive and persecutory light. At this point, it is essential that the relationship with reality be restored—something which requires real effort on the part of the ego, an ego not nourished by dependence. Otherwise, we give the betrayer a position of parasite in our lives, which results in an increasing sense of persecution which we use, paradoxically, to continue to avoid either change or assuming responsibility for ourselves.

The truth is that betrayal is never the fault of just one of the partners. The script followed by both betrayer and betrayed is in some ways a fairly predictable one, in which the most onerous role is reserved for the betrayer, as she must prepare the basis for the revision and dissolving of a relationship that has no more reason to exist. Not uncommonly, although the one betrayed will for some time have had a presentiment of the imminent drama, he will have pretended to suspect nothing because his investment in the other was so total.

There is no end of these soap operas, in which the expression *to love* is—to put it mildly—misused. In fact, it is abused. *To bind* would be more to the point: we bind the other, hand and foot, to our narcissistic dreams. In these situations, the ancient relationship of total dependence on the one who gave us life emerges once more, absolutely unaltered, and there is no degree of "maturity" (which is often nothing more than insensitivity) sufficient to mitigate the resulting pain. For we are dealing here with a relationship with a particular aspect of narcissism. When involved in a passionate love affair, we are convinced of having given our life for our partner, in return for which we received the meaning of life. Our narcissism and self-esteem float out there, among the stars.

It is not clear what is really the cause for one of two partners losing interest, just as it is not clear how one person up to that moment can have been the center of our universe. Why is another, passionately and in entirely unexpected ways, able to arouse sensations the old love no longer can? I believe that the explanation for this lies in the dynamics structured within the relationship: a couple is formed and the two partners interact according to precise patterns; they are, metaphorically speaking, intersecting rings. Often, in fact, the relationship is based on the diversity, rather than the similarity, of the partners. Jung, in this context, used the term *types*. Each partner represents the aspect the other lacks, the part of her personality in shadow. Combined, the two polarities would constitute a whole. Each of the partners seeks completion through the relationship.

In this context, earlier we referred to the hermaphroditic myth in Plato's *Symposium*. A Hebrew analogy is the following passage from the Talmud (Nidda 31, in Elkaim-Sartre 1982):

—Why is it man who seeks woman and not the contrary? asked
the pupils of Rabbi Dostai their master, the son of Rabbi Jani.

—It is as when an object has been lost. Who searches? And for
what do they search? He who has lost something searches for the
object lost.

The lost object here presumably alludes to the rib taken from
Adam while he slept, and the terms *man* and *woman* are not
used so much in their biological as their psychological accepta-
tion. Philo of Alexandria, for example, makes a distinction between the two accounts of the creation of man presented in
Genesis 1.27 and 2.7, to the effect that only the latter (Genesis
2.7: "And the Lord God formed man of the dust of the ground,
and breathed into his nostrils the breath of life; and man became
a living soul.") referred to the male gender, while the former
(Genesis 1.27: "So God created man in his own image, in the
image of God created he him; male and female created he
them.") connotes the human being in his original condition of
indivisibility. According to Philo, the connotation of the latter is
"idea" (with reference to Plato), or "species," while the male and
female genders are connotated as "forms" or "sensitive forms."
As he then writes in *Allegories of Laws* (II.13), God in all things
proceeds in the same manner: in fact, before form He created
genus, as he did thus for man. Having first roughly hewn the
species of man (in which are included, as Moses said, the male
and the female gender), he then produced the sensitive form,
represented by Adam.

We could say that loss—the same loss motivating the incessant
search for the other—is so deeply rooted as to precede conscious human life; that is, the individual's reawakening from the
torpor instigated by God. Loss would therefore appear to be the
actual basis of the relationship. Relationship—in particular the
passionate relationship—is in fact characterized by the idea of
fusion. The fantasy of constituting a unity, or—as we said
previously—feeling that our identity is lost when the other is absent, is the hub around which the love dynamic rotates.

Another implication of this fusional grasping is that, in the relationship, the partners recognize each other only in proportion
to the degree that each fulfills the other's needs. Therefore,

certain patterns of behavior or compulsions are structured in each couple relationship, and it is exclusively upon these patterns that the dynamics of that relationship are based. It is interesting to observe that the causes of rancor and incomprehension between two partners are always the same and remain the same for years—at times an entire lifetime—without a real solution ever being found. If, however, one partner is accepted only insofar as he corresponds to the other's expectations, then clearly both partners are imprisoned in certain roles.

Betrayal therefore must be seen not only as one partner's abandonment of the other, but also as the angry attempt to recognize those parts of himself the relationship has suffocated. If the fantasy of fusion is the cause of each partner having in some way lost her identity and, consequently, her own confines, then betrayal becomes the attempt to reestablish them. Through betrayal it is possible to understand the internal psychological motivations binding us to a certain person, because betrayal represents a point of external observation, one separate from the relationship in question. The most salient aspects of the personality that were placed in shadow in the relationship with the partner can reemerge and be manifested in another relationship.

On closer observation, the personality of the betrayer's new interest will often be revealed to be considerably different from that of the person previously loved and more similar to the personality of the betrayer. For this reason, I consider betrayal a symbolic representation, an inevitable passage in the life of the lovers: an aspect of external and internal opening and the reconquest of individual identity. I also believe that lending an attentive ear to our own fantasies of betrayal is quite a different thing from acting them out impulsively, without reflection. All the hostile impulses that emerge during the course of a relationship should therefore be understood on the conscious level before being acted upon. Otherwise, what will be produced is an enormous quantity of useless suffering. We must be able to discern the emotional and psychological quality of the desire to betray the partner: does the betrayal truly correspond to a phase of growth, or is it an expression of destructive, vindictive, and infantile confusion?

In any case, the devastation caused by betrayal can last for years. Think of the sexual images we carry within us. Every psychologist knows that often the sexual potential of a man or a woman is not nondifferentiated, but bound to a specific individual. Of course, this can also be considered to be positive, a sign of a deep and total involvement. However, when the affair is over—as analytical experience confirms—impotence or frigidity will not infrequently (and sometimes for years) become the companions of the one abandoned.

It is possible that each of us can regress to some specific aspect in our infantile sexual memory, which is reactivated by an encounter. The very common expression, "I feel very drawn to him (or her)" is very apt in this sense, because in these situations we feel literally dragged, captured, unable to free ourselves. This is a dramatic aspect of the couple experience, because it renders us as dependent on the partner as an addict on drugs. Images which captivate us, key images, images which attract (a certain smile, a gesture, a sinuous body, sensuality, the tone of a voice or a pair of lips, any particular characteristic of the partner) have the same arcane power over us that the music of the Pied Piper had on the children of Hamelin.

Fortunately, sooner or later, everything must end. Therefore, if love must inevitably end, so must the pain of abandonment. If we manage to survive this devastating experience and assume responsibility for ourselves, truly appropriating the most beautiful aspects of our union with the man or woman loved, then primary trust will gradually be restored. We cannot know exactly when the next betrayal will occur, but we will at least have learned to recognize it. Without the certainty that we will either bear up better next time or avoid disaster, we can only hope that one day, we will experience once more that love fusion with another partner, in the quest for that paradise lost for having broken its rules.

Eleven

The Compulsion to Seduce and the Advantage of Being Betrayed

No! Let fools make a virtue of constancy! All beautiful women have a right to our love.
                                    —Moliere, *Don Juan*

Jealousy will inevitably make its entrance on the tumultuous stage of betrayal. And there was a precedent for that jealousy—a sentiment which excludes all logic or rationality—during the immediate postbirth phase when, upon realizing that the first love object belonged to someone else, the infant was immediately engaged in a contest with the father for the mother's love. This psychic condition is dredged up from unconscious memory in the adult couple relationship, leading to an obsessive search for the corpus delicti. The behavior and relational capacity of an individual who up to that point may not have been jealous are suddenly transformed. Habitual rationality, self-control, and dignity are swept away in an explosion of violent emotion. When the dimension of passionate love, apparently perfect to the point of seeming otherworldly, unexpectedly becomes betrayal, we become locked into the pain of solitude.

At this point, suspicion, which is an eminently human sentiment in relationship as well as in that moderately paranoic inclination which ensured our survival, becomes morbid and as an obsessive symptom invades our existence. It is unimportant whether or not jealousy is objectively justified. In fact, there is a stubborn resistance against any confutation or reconsideration. We scrutinize the other for signs confirming our suspicions although, consciously, we do not want that confirmation. But, at that point, the die is cast and reality no longer has a role in the game. The interior world moves, radically changing our perception of events, and the same significance is assigned to any number of instances. The ego succumbs to the overwhelming power of the unconscious, and we become emotionally impotent, deprived of all authority, incapacitated and enslaved by suspicion. We are literally at the mercy of persecution fantasies and self-contempt. The reciprocal possession that once nourished us now enslaves us. We are no longer able to relate objectively to the facts, which are interpreted in a single, obsessive perspective, serving only to further confirm our suspicions.

Why this devastation? Apart from the many common clichés used and fatalistic attitudes frequently taken as regards these situations—which, incidentally, reveal the existence of a collective desire to exorcise the specter of the rejected individual—there is one less obvious aspect which could be of interest to us here: it is not the confirmation of our suspicions that annihilates us, but the images which constellated the relationship.

When jealousy replaces love in the relationship with someone with whom we have shared so much, memories of shared moments of happiness become images that imprison and torment us and from which we will never be free. In the shock of realization that those moments are lost forever, we forget the difficulties, the incomprehension, the many small betrayals with which the way to the final break was strewn. We are imprisoned by images: an expression, a movement of the hands, anything (all of which are insignificant to an outside observer, but cherished treasures for the lover). Jealousy recalls these interiorized images, and we are unable to separate them from the libidinal investment which alone created them; for, if we did, we could no longer fantasize the triangle including the third party who now enjoys them. When we feel that we have lost control over the other, the relationship has already ended. We scrutinize his expressions, search his pockets and wallet, read his diaries, notice every change in his dress, interpreting silences and words alike. Trust has disappeared forever. Unfortunately, however, suspicions are never formed in a vacuum, and although there may have been no concrete betrayal as yet, the jealous intuition is usually justified. The primary trust which made possible our passionate love has been compromised and, if the relationship survives, it does so for other reasons.

One more aspect we might mention—and one which cannot be understood by one devoured by jealousy—is that the accusation of betrayal is often indistinguishable from the projection of the accuser's own desire to betray. In other words, the jealous individual unconsciously cultivates her own fantasy of betrayal to demonstrate her own autonomy. It is clear that that reaction is to paralyzing dependence, in this case reinforced by the condition of having been rejected. We fear betrayal above all because we desire it. In the couple relationship, there is an irresistible reciprocal need to control, and the intensity of that need is in proportion to the extent to which the dynamics of that relationship are based on neurotic collusion. And, although the condition of neurotic collusion can be a resistant basis, it can also be an extremely fragile one. The other's violation of the pact can be the catalyst forcing us to come to terms with our own illness. How often does a man conceal his own depression from himself by experiencing it surreptitiously, through the depression of his wife, boycotting any attempt at healing, plunging headlong into an interior vacuum when the relationship fails! As there are usually no plausible pretexts for exercising control over the other, it is jealousy which will provide an excellent excuse for conduct otherwise unacceptable.

There are also those who constantly, and with varying degrees of awareness, assume a seductive attitude aimed at arousing jealousy, as if that were the only existential condition possible for them. This type of individual seduces compulsively, in order to feel alive. What is the origin of this need? The psychology of the jealous person is not all that different from the psychology of the person who continually provokes it. In fact when the two types meet they often unite to form couples.

The potentially jealous individual falls in love with someone irrepressibly driven to put him to the test, just as the betrayer needs a jealous person to control and contain his tendency to betray. This is one example of neurotic collusion, an attraction based on a pathological interplay which is binding to the extent that it is experienced unconsciously. The desire to betray conceals an insatiable thirst for confirmation; self-esteem has never been consolidated, and consequently the need for daily affective and erotic reassurance is created. In these conditions, it would be misleading to speak of "love"; individuals with this kind of existential equilibrium cause great suffering in all those unfortunate enough to fall into their net. But are there psychological advantages to being betrayed? If so, what are they exactly? One would be the identification of the betrayed person with a masochistic position, and another the opportunity the betrayal provides for him to negate his excessive need for transgression and his own sensuality.

What we are dealing with here is a sort of psychological tropism, in which two people industriously weave a web of deceit, control, and suspicion. Don Juan is the most familiar literary illustration of this dynamic; a man in flight, absolutely incapable of maintaining an authentic relationship. He is the classic seducer, constantly in search of a new woman in whom to inspire hope, which he will then literally and inevitably dash. However, because he inspires that hope, he is intensely loved. The reason for this is that the woman has conserved, from earliest infancy, an unsatisfied need for mirroring. She aspires to become the object of the man's dedication, comprehension, and respect.

However, besides being loved, the man is also hated as he is absolutely incapable of satisfying the woman's needs and will inevitably betray and abandon her. Another literary example of this type is Frederic Moreau in Flaubert's *Sentimental Education* (Miller 1981). An analysis of this character reveals that the seducer would, in all probability, have been convinced as a child that any rebellion against his mother would result in her immediately abandoning him. There are, in fact, extremely fragile maternal figures who, expecting a maximum effort of adjustment from their children, threaten to abandon them the moment they succeed in saying no. These children, as adults, will neurotically attempt to transform into action that same dynamic by offering gratification and admiration to women and then suddenly withdrawing it. Betrayal constitutes one of the most searing wounds of this attitude, which reveals a liberty that is only apparent. That "liberty," in fact, conceals the deep dependence of an individual who is not allowed to say no because mother would never have permitted it. Naturally, this delayed and deflected retaliation, directed toward other female creatures for the suffering inflicted on the seducer by that first and most powerful feminine figure in life, will never even the score and end the game.

The problem of Don Juan, according to Otto Rank, is actually a secret, unconscious conspiracy to be faithful to an unattainable, irreplaceable mother. And not even the enormous number of women he constantly and compulsively seduces will succeed in neutralizing so powerful a figure (Rank 1922). Rank also writes (ibid.):

> The continually repeated sexual conquest of woman remains unsatisfactory, for the reason that the infantile tendency to regress to the mother can only be partially fulfilled.

We could reverse that assumption, as in fact Rank does, to the effect that it was the women who actually conquered Don Juan and not the other way around. This is made evident in his interpretation of Edmond Rostand's dramatic poem, "The Last Night of Don Juan," published posthumously, in 1921, in which Rank describes the culminating moment as follows:

> The devil, who increasingly takes over the role of Don Juan's own conscience, puts him to a test. The test consists of recognizing the soul of a particular woman from a few whispered words, for Don Juan denied that he only recognized the woman's body.

Thus, according to Rostand, the price paid by Don Juan was his total incapacity to recognize the soul. We could ask at this point whether or not Don Juan actually learned anything from his human, all too human, career of seducer. According to Rank (ibid.),

> he has known only masks: always they have lied to him, and he himself wanted those lies, for the woman appears to the man as he wishes her to be . . . the women conquered him, and if he left them, it was because the unadmitted fear of having to remain with one of them drove him to it.

We all carry the scars of childhood. However, an unhealed wound does not belong entirely to the past, for it remains constantly present, demanding to be dressed and drained. And, over the long term—sometimes a lifetime—that repetition-compulsion will dominate the affective relationships of the survivors of that conflict, the wounds of which, although inflicted in a distant past, are still fresh. Congenial to this compulsion is a typical strategy of the seducer: lying. In order to "spare" the women frustration and disappointment—as the child he was with his mother—he seeks refuge from one woman with the successive one, all the while telling lies. Suffocated by a woman's increasingly pressing requests, he will attempt to regain his freedom by provoking her to become cruel. But his will be an indirect provocation, for the drama of the seducer lies in his incapacity to express his needs directly.

As a result, he is cast into a deep sorrow, which explodes when the woman unmasks his hypocrisy. The more vindictively the woman reacts to the insult of his deception, the more the seducer feels justified in abandoning her, thus once more illuding himself at having gained a certain distance from his mother. He will then approach another partner, thus perpetuating the diabolic cycle of gratification and disappointment. As comprehensive and affectionate as the new partner may be, she is destined, like Don Quixote, to do battle with windmills, because she can never possess the power necessary to cancel out the event of the original trauma that made the seducer what he is. And he, in the most unconscious and subtle way, will force her to renounce comprehension for cruelty. According to Alice Miller (1981), the cowardice of Frederic Moreau conceals a tragedy. In the same context, the fact that someone has succeeded in growing up sincere and open presumably will depend on the degree of tolerance his parents had as regards the truth as well as the sanctions they imposed on him.

There can be no passionate relationship without jealousy or betrayal. Jealousy expresses the right over another, a primitive possession that overrides reason and can on occasion lead to criminal action. However, this mechanism can also be present— and far more frequently than is generally thought—in the very sensitive dimension of incest.

Twelve

The Climate of Incest

The expression, too violent, too hard to pronounce or to hear, is curbed. There are no words to express it. Violence by the father does not exist; it is impossible. It was she who seduced him. A father cannot "sin" in that way; it would be too detestable. Too much! And so, it is not mentioned.

The father is law! . . . The father is the moral guarantor. The father is family; he is sacred and beyond reproach. He is a pillar of society. If he falls, everything is lost, all values: country, work, family. Thus, the adolescent and her truth are silenced forever.

—E. Thomas, *Le viol du silence*

Incest is the dimension that prevents experiencing passion outside the family circle. It also represents so drastic a transgression of accepted psychic and social patterns than even mention of it is avoided, even though it constitutes one of the most sinister and cruel of all betrayals. Ferenczi, a student of Freud's, wrote an article in 1932 on a very particular form of communication between the language of the child and the language of the adult, in which infantile intention—for example that of a little girl caressing her father—is betrayed by the morbid perception of the parent.

The different points of view from which Freud and Jung approached the theme of incest are illustrated in two texts, presented almost contemporaneously: Freud's *Totem and Taboo* (1912–1913) and Jung's *Symbols of Transformation* (1912–1952). That difference also represented a symbolic division of sorts in the lives of the two men, as well as in the history of psychoanalytical theory. However, despite the diversity of the two concepts, both make a connection between the dynamics of incest and the universal foundations of most cultures. Both also agree that the prohibition—or, in any case, the overcoming—of the incestuous tendency cleared the way to consciousness and culture. The points of view of Freud and Jung on incest are essential to understanding the absolutely extrinsic and distorted nature of *moralistic* judgment of this transgression, when it should be seen instead as disastrous for the psychological growth of the individual.

There is no culture in which the taboo of incest does not exist, and this could mean that it represents a universal psychic constellation. The theme of the adult seduction of a child is the basis of the theory of the Oedipus complex which, on a phylogenetic level, Freud traces to the totemistic system, and which in neurosis is transformed into unconscious fantasy powerful enough to invade the entire psychic life of the individual. The concept of incestuous fantasies is an important one because it presents the problem expressed in terms not only of reality, but of intimate imagination as well. Taboos are ancient prohibitions and as such *could* be considered part of an innate, natural patrimony. In fact, Freud wrote:

> Who can decide whether such things as "innate ideas" exist, or whether in the present instance they have operated, either alone or in conjunction with education to bring about the permanent fixing of taboos?

According to Freud, group cohesion, which is a prerequisite for civil and cultural development, can be established and maintained only through the prohibition of incest, because only thus will law exercise control over desire and the principle of reality triumph over the pleasure principle. The sublimation of incestuous desires transforms the primitive horde into a society regulated by rules; a society in which cultural organization intervenes on an exclusively biological existence, redefining it. As regards energies, the prohibition of incest creates a deviation of the "endogamous libido," directing it outward, externally, to the social structure, thus encouraging object investment outside the strict family nucleus. Consequently, culture could not exist without the restriction of the endogamous tendency of psychic energy.

Jung saw the problem in a completely different way. In fact, according to his theory, the desire to sleep with the mother or the father must be understood as a symbolic expression of the psyche and a metaphor for psychological development. From this point of view, the taboo of incest would not be the result of external imposition, but a restraint which evolves spontaneously with individual growth. In fact, the prohibition of incest forces the individual to abandon a symbiotic situation with the mother and hypnosis by the unconscious, resulting both in his being freed from his condition of confused collective tribal creature and in the development of self-awareness. Consequently, it was not a real event that inspired the taboo, but the instinct to evolve, integrating the unconscious aspects of the personality, in a process Jung called individuation. The creative potential of our psychic energy is expressed in a exogamic thrust leading us to seek union outside the group, while incestuous desires tend to keep us trapped in original ties. If, as Jung thought, opposing the unconscious endogamous personality is the conscious exogamic personality, then the former—because it is unconscious—will be felt to be extraneous and will emerge in the form of projections. The incestuous endogamic dimension finds its space therefore in fantasy, or else it is projected onto human figures with exclusive prerogatives—kings and princes, for example, as illustrated by the tragedies of Oedipus and Phaedra. In art, the "mystical wedding," or the alchemical representations of the *Hieros Gamos* (the sacred marriage), are symbolic expressions of the psychic tendency toward the union of opposites. Incestuous desire—be it active or passive—is therefore a constant factor of human experience.

What is important then is to understand its symbolic meaning and its role in the evolution of each individual's psychic equilibrium. While, on the one hand, the regressive state into which the incestuous tendency plunges us prevents our emergence from a purely collective existence, on the other it represents the necessary passage of the libido toward the origins, as a prelude to transformation. A symbolic expression of this passage is the hero's abandoning his mother to undertake a voyage in pursuit of his destiny. That voyage usually includes a nocturnal sea crossing, from west to east—from the setting sun to symbolic renaissance. It is a plunge into the depths of the libido, through which the extraordinary mystery of individual existence will be unveiled to him.

In a literal interpretation of incestuous desire, incest does not occur only between mother and son or father and daughter, but also during the analytical process in which the image of a strong father and weak daughter often reemerges, activating incestuous emotions. In that context, respecting the rule of abstinence implies not only the respect of the person and her suffering, but also the authentic and nonpersonalized value of the endogamous drive. Acting out the incestuous fantasy destroys the possibility of experiencing psychic impulse on a symbolic level. When incest is put into action, the daughter or—less frequently—the son is destroyed from within and placed in a condition of no longer disposing of the creative exogamous energy that needs to be carried toward the exterior. When the protective and integrating rituals of the endogamous libido are abandoned, the child is abandoned to herself. She must then, alone, provide the solution to a moral conflict far beyond her real capacity for elaboration, a conflict involving the most profound mysteries of life. She is rejected and thrown back entirely onto herself because, as she is bound to secrecy as regards other members of the family, she is deprived of those external points of reference indispensable to her during that phase of her biological and psychic development. It requires a very evolved consciousness to psychically survive contact with incest and not fall victim to an inner splitting of the personality.

> I could not scream, for I no longer had a voice. My father had torn out my tongue, hypnotizing me with the strength of his power-love.
> And I remained thus, attempting to gather up my pieces, in a last gesture of hope. Show the skeletal body of a "concentration camp victim" in an attempt to designate the executioner. But no one could understand because the executioner seemed enclosed in the body of his victim. And I could not designate the executioner otherwise, being as I was in his power-love, even though for me the word love—like that of father or lover—had no other

meaning. At night father became lover, and without a word became father once more the day after. The flesh negates the word, subverting its meaning. Meaning is overturned. The word father explodes in contact of the sexes of father and daughter: an impossible, inconceivable contact, an overwhelming loss of references, the sense of the word, the sense of life (Thomas 1986)

The experience of incest causes devastating psychic splitting that also renders impossible any other relationship within the family, thus depriving the child of his basic affective basis. Over the child's need for tenderness and his desire for bodily contact which is necessary at that level of his development, adult violence superimposes a sadistic sexuality with which the child has no possibility of interacting. The affective dimension therefore clearly assumes the connotations of blackmail. If we think of the importance the mirroring function offered by the adult represents for the child, we will have some idea of the internal devastation incest causes. Only by mirroring through empathic comprehension of the child's internal world can the parent help him to name, for the first time, his emotions, needs, and fears.

I believe that many women conceal some event connected to their psychosexual development, inevitably related to an outrage—although possibly less manifest than incest. For this reason, women usually possess that characteristic sensitivity which men lack.

Imprisoning the daughter in the concrete expression of the relationship with the real and personal father will precondition her future sexual and sentimental life. In fact, the wound of incest often results in a defensive process in which Eros is split from sexuality, in the sense that sentiments of love, tenderness, and intimacy do not, as is usual in adult relationships, accompany the sexual experience. The consequence of this wound is a seriously compromised Eros and an incapacity to form relationships with the diverse, both in intrapsychic terms (for example, nonintegrated polarity) and in the sphere of a real relationship with another individual. By separating sex from sentiment, the child (and later on the adult), marked by the incestuous experience, avoids experiencing feelings of guilt:

Love cannot be torture. I am convinced of having found a good mother, and I find myself shortly afterward before an executioner who I cannot leave. It is from that hell that I have come, that skin of a victim I so painfully tear away.

How did it happen? Images run through my head.

The photograph of my father holding me as a newborn child on his knee, childhood photographs, wedding photographs, communion photographs, photographs of Daddy beside his daughter.

A father's tenderness for his daughter, the kisses at bedtime, the cuddles, Daddy's knee, daily tenderness. The father's authoritative glance, the authority of father-tenderness. That tenderness as necessary as food for survival. If he does not love me, he could kill me. (Thomas 1986)

I repeat: the problem is more serious from a psychological than a moral point of view, because in these cases the creativity associated with Eros is blocked by repression. And the primitive shattering of love, by means of which the affective element is split from the instinctive one, will affect the child's entire life. Sexuality has meaning only when accompanied by sentiment. If the first sexual experience is incest, there will be space only for fear.

It is so beautiful outside, and here I am behind closed shutters, reading books about others doing the opposite, and which I am unable to do.

I have determined the importance, the necessity, but my brain will not function, and my body will not advance. And so, I content myself with reading descriptions, novels narrating lost childhood. It is above all thanks to Sheila MacLeod's book on her anorexic experience that I was able to break the glass prison in which I lived with my pieces scattered about. It was a transparent prison, my invisible protection against others, and my prison which had become me to confront the world was useful in keeping together all my pieces.

Now that I have shattered that protection, of which I was not conscious, I no longer know how to communicate with others, because I am not familiar with this woman's body of mine, finally gathered together, reunited. (Thomas 1986)

That description, by a woman who was raped as a child by her father, is an excellent illustration of the dramatic splitting that results in the body being experienced without feeling—

something similar to eating without being hungry. In the life of that woman, every sexuality-related aspect will be marked by that violent breach of trust. When the tension between the endogamous libido and its prohibition is not sufficient to deflect it toward the exterior, which alone makes possible an object investment, we are exiled not only from the world, but from ourselves.

> Better to die than be my father's prohibited object of desire! He destroyed me, flung me into hell. I chose the way of heaven, becoming a kind of luminous angel that returned towards God-life, despite him, despite them, despite the curate and the nuns. Terrestrial life was forbidden me, and so I chose another life, the way of the soul, purification through abstinence, initiation: a mystic delirium of sorts.
>
> I could not be what I had chosen alone, in my own mind, in the mirror of the future; my father had destroyed that with his sex. And so there was nothing left for me but the way of non-being, the way of death. (Thomas 1986)

That father-tenderness was a perverse individual, a rapist, incestuous, despicable. And there are hundreds like him—tender, gentle fathers who attack and rape their daughters in the silence of the night, in a basement, in a forest, in the parents' double bed. But the world remains silent, suffocating their cries which will never be heard, betraying them and consigning them to a soundless vacuum. Family and honor are to be saved at all costs. And then, as the damage is already done, what would be the point of making matters worse? Prison for the father, shame for the entire family. And what would happen to the other children without a father to feed them? Better be still, pretending to have seen nothing, understood nothing, as if it were all a dream. And, of course, it could also have been a dream, because all daughters dream of sleeping with their fathers. And so, the little girl is convinced that by talking she would destroy her entire family.

Thirteen

An Unfrequented Temple

*Nobody would choose to live without friends even if he
had all the other good things.*

—Aristotle, *Etichs*

In his *Philosophical Dictionary* (1764), Voltaire observed that
friendship in our culture had become "by now a temple seldom
frequented." And, in fact, most positive evaluations of friendship
will be found either in the past or in other cultures—Arab,
Greek, and biblical, for example. The cultural and popular tradi-
tions most familiar to us generally express little enthusiasm for
that particular affective tie. Famous maxims and anonymous
proverbs will more likely express mistrust of friendship than
praise it. Even on those rare occasions that friendship is considered a value to be preserved, it is usually as something optional.

Very often we will hear an individual say that friendship—for
lack of time or because she is dedicated to some noble pursuit—
is a luxury she cannot permit herself. This kind of person (more
often a man than a woman), who is committed, in varying degrees, to some task or mission will continue, doggedly and
undistracted, in pursuit of some objective. The result of that obsession is usually a decrease in the capacity to relate to others.
In fact, many successful professionals are not very effective in
their interpersonal relationships precisely because all their energies are absorbed by that demon urging them on. It would seem
they had no interests in life beyond that objective, and the price
they pay is isolation: the lack of friendships and solidarity. It is
interesting to note that these individuals will usually consider
any suggestion that they direct their attention elsewhere, even

temporarily, a sinister threat to their appointed destiny. Kracauer (1971, 69–70) writes, apropos of this type of man:

> The effort to create absorbs him, demands all his strength and, should he decide to withdraw from that task in order to enjoy the sweetness of soul to soul effusion, it would be considered a betrayal.

Totally incapable of existing in an uneventful space or time, these individuals, pursued by a void, will usually be absent from the collective scene, avoiding any form of participation or involvement. In fact, the inability to identify with the group is characteristic of this type of personality. And that mechanism, which has been rooted in the human psyche from time immemorial, is essential because it functions as a constant mediator between the individual and his human environment and is functional to status and acquiring a sense of security.

Conversely, the implications of assimilation into a group are not always positive. For, while that assimilation reinforces the individual, it also devalues him by depriving him of his distinguishing aspect, his subjective difference. However, the opposite is also true; an individual will often attempt to conform when she perceives the diversity of others as a threat.

On occasion, a particular field is created within a group when two people begin to reserve a more limited space for themselves, within which psychological understanding is formed. It is not obvious why this occurs. An individual's process of differentiating himself from the group psychology will often result in the need for a psychological relationship to substitute the previous identification with the collective. That privileged encounter is generally perceived as irrational, apparently without motivation, but then any important encounter has its mysterious and ineffable aspects. For such an encounter is a rare event and different from many other chance emotional involvements (for example, an unexpected confession, often the result of a nondifferentiated attempt to unveil an interior dimension, but not reciprocal—that is, with no realistic expectation of response). However, while there is greater intimacy in other relationships (love, for example, which of itself does not exclude the psychological dimension of friendship), I consider relationships between individuals of the same sex the most fertile ground for friendship as a conscious relationship. In that type of relationship, the other becomes the occasion for a conscious dialogic relationship with ourselves and that which is different from us.

Friendship, in fact, forces us to elaborate, not always successfully, a series of specific difficulties. The effort necessary for that elaboration, aptly expressed by Theognis as the attempt to temper our own nature to the nature of friends, takes on the connotations of a need for transformation through the creation of profound contact with the parts of the Self (Theognis, vv. 213–218). Theognis also describes this self-exploration as similar to the camouflaging of the nature of the many-tentacled polyp to the nature of the rock on which it is attached. In other words, wisdom is worth more than intransigence. The observation attributed to Theognis becomes even more interesting if compared to another from the same collection, according to which the division between friendship and betrayal is slight, because the qualities possessed by the friend and those characterizing the betrayer are merely two sides of the same coin. Also, many people have deceitful natures, but their changeable souls conceal them. However, according to Theognis, sooner or later everyone's nature is revealed. Other venerable maxims mention, for example, that "a man is fortunate if he has encountered so much as the shadow of a friend" (Menander), or that "he who finds a friend finds a treasure" (Ecclesiastes).

On the psychological level, we can understand this to mean that, while the desire for relationship is innate, the capacity to create and maintain one is acquired. In the final analysis, the love experience was originally a consequence of the *biological* instinct for reproduction, while friendship is a matter of *culture*, part of the psychological field within which events move inevitably toward a conclusion that is also of a psychological nature. In evaluating an individual's psychic equilibrium, not only should his affective and professional life be observed, but also the existence and quality of his friendships. In life, while friends are few, casual companions with whom we share a brief passage, the destination of which we are already aware, are many. Relationships with acquaintances, colleagues, fellow students, good-time buddies, comrades-in-arms, or compatriots are substantially different from friendship, because they are based on common intent, which is clearly defined and circumscribed. Also, working together toward a common objective tends to have a leveling effect on personality differences, preventing reciprocal involvement in extraneous matters, which could introduce uncontrolled variables into the group's functioning. Of course, this does not exclude the possibility that, between acquaintances, one may be willing to lay down her life for another. In the psychological context, however, the drive investment involved there is less in the companion than in the collective ideal.

Aristotle made a distinction between friendship based on utilitarian or sexual objectives from the relationship in which friends are loved for their character, their essence, their soul. In the latter, there can also be some sexual or physical trace; however, it will be secondary. For it is a bond uniting soul to soul. The homosexual implications in some, or perhaps all, friendships should not be condemned as a perversion of the relationship; as Jung observed, sexuality is not only one of the soul's the most powerful symbols, and therefore possibly the vehicle for other meanings—it also represents one of the fundamental mediators of our existence. We may all have heard the phrases, "love without sexuality but not without body" (Guggenbühl-Craig) or "spiritualized erotic love," and it is common knowledge that the choice of friends is also based on physical attraction. This was understood very well by Aristotle, who recognized in intimacy a decisive factor in friendship. In his *Etichs*, he bases the choice of friends, no less than the choice of a lover, on feeling (Aristotle, *Etichs* 1171):

> Are we to say, then, that just as lovers find the keenest satisfaction in seeing, and prefer this sense to all the others, because they feel that it is the source and stay of love, so to friends there is nothing more desirable than spending their lives together? For friendship is a kind of partnership, and a man stands in the same relation to his friend as to himself.

Consequently, the realization of that experience can only occur in intimacy. Aristotle concludes his observation as follows (ibid.):

and since the consciousness of his own existence is desirable, the consciousness of his friend's must be the same; and this consciousness becomes actualized in their life together, so that they naturally desire it.

An authentic psychological relationship requires a deep and conscious acceptance of the other, which also includes his less noble aspects. Tolerance and deep compassion, in the etymological sense of "experiencing together," means above all that we have accepted *our own* negative aspect; the Shadow which is our constant companion. Only thus will we succeed in guaranteeing lasting affection to a friend despite her imperfect humanity, which counters our desire to idealize. Otherwise, she will be no more than an echo of our own narcissism, and those elements resembling us will nourish us, as a continual confirmation of ourselves.

Clearly, if we have placed complete trust in the other, in this case as well, betrayal can occur with devastating effects. Such a situation is described in Sophocles' tale of the mythical hero, Philoctetes. That personage, after being bitten on the foot by a snake, is abandoned by the Greeks on the deserted island of Lemnos, because his wound "plagues the air and his racking cries are a torment to his companions." Since it had been prophesied that Troy could not be conquered without the bow of Philoctetes, Odysseus, Neoptolemus, and the son of Achilles land on Lemnos, intent on stealing the bow. Odysseus realizes that, as that would be impossible using force or persuasion, they must use deceit. And the deception proposed by Odysseus to Neoptolemus includes betrayal: Neoptolemus must first win the unconditional friendship and confidence of Philoctetes and, once certain of his trust, steal the bow. In fact, that is how it goes—at least initially. It is interesting to note here that in the passage Sophocles attributes to the betrayed hero there is an inversion of logic, as characteristic as it is significant. The hero exclaims (Sophocles, *Philoctetes*, v. 923), "I am dead, betrayed!" thus connoting betrayal as a condition subsequent to death; a more disastrous condition than death itself.

The effects of betrayal are far more devastating when it is friends who betray. Often, however, betrayal is a defensive reaction to the disappointment of the narcissistic expectations mentioned above. A differentiated relationship goes beyond symbiotic gratification and presupposes assuming the responsibility of our own Shadow. We could flee from it by projecting it onto a friend, but that would only postpone the challenge. Contrary to what occurs in the love relationship, in friendship there is an additional possibility of surviving betrayal, by seizing its propulsive aspects and not permitting the destructive aspect to reach the point of destroying the relationship. Betrayal can thus be the occasion for reestablishing the relationship on the basis of a deeper and broader comprehension. We may never unveil ourselves to our life-companion as completely as we do to a friend of our own sex.

Female friendship is often more solid than friendship between men, in which rivalry and violence pollute the relationship to a far greater degree. In friendship between women, not only affection, but also its demonstration through physical contact, are permissible; walking together arm in arm, or greetings with affectionate kisses, for example. The same comportment in men is practically unacceptable in Western cultures (whereas in Arab countries, the rules are quite different). The fact that the demonstration of affection between men is not condoned by our culture is due not only to a different experiencing of the body, but also a different kind of acceptance of the other, the friend. While negative aspects must often be hidden even from lovers, they can be revealed before friends. Friendship has been compared to a relationship between two souls, for it is in that relationship that we can experience deep spirituality. Greek poetry abounds in examples of sacrifice for the sake of friendship. If we accept the other's diversity, friendship can be stimulating because that diversity will open the way to other dimensions of existence. In any case, love—or Eros as the capacity to relate—is based on that acceptance of the irreducibility of those close to us.

It is perhaps in the context of that irreducibility that the parable of the Rabbi, in Cohen's exposition of the Talmud, should be understood (1932):

Rabbinical teaching on brotherly love is no finer synthesis than the incisive epigram: "Who is powerful? He who makes a friend of an enemy."

It is extremely difficult for parents to recognize the diversity of the children to whom they have given life. Their belief that they are owed something by their children (common also in those who claim to believe that life is a gift, but from God) is revealing as to the idea those parents have of their own role. In friendship, the additional possibility of giving space to the diversity of the other provides an element of psychological enrichment; through a friend we see the world in a way *not habitual* to us, which for that very reason can be very attractive, in a situation in which we will probably be willing to risk more. The friend is a mirror of the other's soul, his self. Remember the saying, "Tell me who your friends are, and I will tell you who you are." If I succeed in giving my soul to the other and he succeeds in accepting it, then I am mirrored in him, as he is in me.

There is a religious quality underlying friendship. A possible religious etymon—proposed for example by Christianity—considered *friendship* as meaning "getting together, being together"; in fact, it is through friends that we discover that deep communication which enriches us. In difficult moments, it is the friendless who feel truly alone.

In Greek tragedy, the redeeming expedient leading to the resolution of the drama is the famous *deus ex machina*—which, translated onto the personal level, would be the intervention of friends, perceived as something religious, something absolutely gratuitous, the *longa manus* of a god. The possibility of receiving this help in no way constitutes an obstacle to our development. Moreover, in certain circumstances, asking for help and accepting it implies an awareness of our intrinsic fragility, a sure sign of psychological maturity. While the problem there is recognizing our own impotence, the problem of many psychologists—who as such should be psychologically more evolved than the average person—is their occasional belief that they are omnipotent. Remember the biblical phrase, "Ask and ye shall receive." Never asking, rather than implying complete self-sufficiency, is a pathology.

In the Talmud (Berakhoth 5b in Elkaim-Sartre 1982), there is a tale that is revealing in this context: One day, Rabbi Johanan fell ill, at which point Rabbi Hanina paid him a visit and asked him if he was capable of bearing willingly the punishment inflicted on him. Receiving a decidedly negative response, Rabbi Hanina asked Rabbi Johanan to give him his hand. Rabbi Johanan did so and was healed. At this point the question posed by the Talmudic tale is why could Rabbi Johanan not heal himself, and the response is referred to the conclusion of the subsequent tale, which exactly repeats the first. Rabbi Hiya then falls ill and, this time, it is Rabbi Johanan who comes to see him and asks him if he is able to bear willingly the punishment inflicted. This time as well, after receiving a negative response, Rabbi Johanan asks him to give him his hand. Rabbi Hiya does so and is healed. Apparently, Rabbi Hiya was also incapable of healing himself. Why? Why was he unable to heal himself? And the Talmud (ibid.) responds thus: "Because a prisoner cannot free himself."

A prisoner cannot free herself alone. Perhaps being a prisoner is the natural condition of everyone, and, consequently, no one can expect to free herself unaided, in the same way that no one—to use another expression from the Talmud—can expect to heal herself. Paradoxically, the surest sign of endless imprisonment is declaring oneself to be self-sufficient.

As we have said, friendship—contrary to love—is not exclusively motivated by biological instinct, but exclusively by the desire for relationship with another human being. True friendship is exclusive; it involves sentiments of abandonment and inspires jealousy and envy in those who are spectators and not protagonists. Think of the hostility so commonly felt by parents toward their children's friends whom they believe are leading their children astray. Because friendship normally involves idealizing the other, a friend's betrayal can be even more painful than a lover's. Disappointment in real friendship can ruin a person's life; in fact, a friendship is more difficult to reconstruct than a love relationship. In friendship, therefore, we must explain, revealing our own human dimension, precisely because the other tends to idealize us.

114

Fourteen

Sex Negated

*Marriages are common throughout nature, since all
species include the male and the female. The trees and
the buds—even rocks and stones—couple.*
—Luther, *Discourses*

In the first of his *Odes*, Pindar wrote:

Son of Tantalus, in my tale of you
I shall counter the poets before me.
When your father called his companions
To his most innocent banquet, and to Sypylos his home,
Making the Gods his guests, who had made him theirs,
Then the bright Trident's God
Lost his heart for love of you, and seized you,
And carried you on his golden mares
To the high house of wide-worshipped Zeus:
Where later in time Ganymede came also
For the same service to Zeus.

The service referred to by Pindar alludes to the love relationship
between two gods, Poseidon and Zeus, and two mythical personages, Pelops, son of Tantalus and progenitor of the Atridae, and
Ganymede, the most beautiful of living youths. Therefore, myth
in a certain sense legitimizes the homosexual union in paradise.
However, in the passage from ancient Greece to the modern era,
also as a result of the decisive mediation of newer Christian values, that legitimist attitude gradually metamorphosed, to the point
of becoming, for the most part, the opposite.

A film adaption was made in 1971 of E. M. Forster's novel,
Maurice, the tale of a young man who, together with a contemporary, discovers his own homosexuality. The action of the

film—which remains faithful to the novel—takes place in the classic context of an English private school. Written in the Victorian era, the novel was only published posthumously, because the author himself had considered its publication unthinkable, in the sense that it would have caused the same reactions it described. Be that as it may, we cannot exclude the possibility that the author's decision—apart from his acute perception that the book's happy ending, infinitely more provocative than the theme itself, would have aroused strong reactions—was also motivated by his own feelings of shame and guilt. The central element of the encounter in the novel was a sensuality without platonic posturing or disguise, in defiance of prevailing literary etiquette. In his brief preface, Forster wrote that the man in the street does not abhor so much the fact in itself (in this case, homosexuality), as the "inducement to consider it."

If, in fact, homosexuality were legalized overnight and without excessive fuss, there would be no imposing of taboos or defensive reaction, because it would simply have been inserted normally into the social order of things, and no one would give it another thought. The perversion is not individual, but social, because it is society that stubbornly refuses to accept a reality which has always been part of the human community. The existence of homosexuality was recorded as far back as third-dynasty Egypt (2500 B.C.), in the Old Testament (together with the comment that its practice was punishable by death), in ancient Hittite law (1400 B.C.), which permitted marriage between persons of the same sex, and of course in ancient Greece and Rome. We might comment at this point that a contemporary parallel to the Hittite culture exists only in California, the most liberal state in the United States as regards sexual custom—the homosexual couple was legally recognized in California in 1984 (Di Meglio 1990).

In contemporary Western society, what permitted the collective repression of homoerotic problems was the almost total absence of psychological studies and advanced research on the subject. Our culture would apparently be reasonably informed as to the patriarchal canons in force in Christianity and previously in the Hebrew culture, condemning out of hand anything besides the accepted model of virility. Apart from man-in-the-

116

street opinion, the environment of homosexuality is perfect for our discourse on betrayed sexuality.

Everyone is born with a genetically and physiologically determined sexual identity (with a few chromosomal exceptions) and, for reasons intrinsic to the survival of the species, the most common orientation is heterosexual. Love for the same sex would consequently be *contra naturam*. And yet, it is legitimate to suppose that the cultural system representing an evolved passage is by now the "natural" protraction of the biological organism, and therefore something far more radical than a simple superstructure. As a consequence, human sexuality cannot be entirely explained as the means to merely biological ends, particularly when we consider the fact that erotic sensitivity persists well beyond the strictly fertile period.

However, it is also true that feeling attracted to someone does not necessarily imply an awakening of the procreative instinct, which in any case also requires a reasonable psychological relationship. Sexuality for the most part takes the form of desire for another, and the sex of that person can be absolutely irrelevant to the satisfaction of that natural need. Consider the theory advanced by Kenneth Dover in his study on homosexuality in ancient Greece, keeping in mind that in classical Greek there were no terms corresponding to our *heterosexual* and *homosexual*— which paradoxically owe their existence to Greek morphemes. Kenneth Dover starts out with the reasonable assumption that homosexuality, so widespread in ancient Greece, "satisfied a need not otherwise adequately satisfied within Greek society" (Dover 1978, 211):

> It seems to me that the need in question was a need for personal relationships of an intensity not commonly found within marriage or in the relations between parents and children or in those between the individual and the community as a whole.

Consequently, motivating the homosexual choice in ancient Greece was the need for a more intense relationship. We know that "in Crete as in Sparta, pederast relationships were . . . an integral part of the system of educating adolescents" (Calame 1977, 75). These relationships, continues Calame (ibid.), which existed only between adolescents and older men already solidly

117

integrated in the adult order, had a didactic function: they guaranteed that the loved one conformed to the model represented by the lover; that is, he assimilated gradually, through imitation, the qualities of the perfect citizen.

Also according to Dover, in Eros-idealizing Greek literature, the most relevant aspect of those relationships was not the physical act. Instead, it was a relationship of mutual devotion and sacrifice, which also included emulation and the awakening of sensitivity, imagination, and intellect (Dover 1973).

Starting off with this premise, therefore, can we speak of betrayed sexuality in the sphere of homosexual relationships? As we anticipated, this assumption is rooted the same collective prejudice that from time to time forces various minorities into the role of scapegoat. And how often are those desiring a companion of the same sex plunged into the same psychological dimension characteristic of minorities in the midst of differently oriented groups. Homosexuality then is less a betrayal of nature than a divergence from social custom. The broader society relegates diversity to clandestinity and shame, consequently making those who deviate the potential prey of social aggressiveness. Homosexuality offends not only nature, but conscience as well—conscience as the elective environment in which the betrayal of nature is consumed.

Think of Pasolini, against whom the accusation of homosexuality was used (as usual) to devalue his spirit, his soul. Our greatness will never be recognized if in our deepest and most vital parts we nurture dreams, drives, and affective projects with which the majority are not willing to identify. Freud was among the first to approach this problem in psychological terms. However, admittedly, neither his interpretation nor those that followed have yet succeeded in providing anything approaching an exhaustive explanation of the homosexual choice. Perhaps this is because we have only recently emerged from the atmosphere of the witch hunt. At that time, paradoxically, homosexuality was considered a psychological disturbance, and homosexuals were at least protected from legal measures. Only in 1974 did the American DSM (*Diagnostic and Statistical Manual of Mental Disorders*) finally remove homosexuality from the list of mental illnesses as a result of the Kinsey Report of 1948, which revealed that 40 percent of American adult males had experienced one complete homosexual intercourse.

Homosexuality, like any other form of "perversion," must be seen as a *particular and specific way of encountering the love experience.* We cannot comprehend homosexuality if we separate it from love. And clinical experience leads inevitably to the conclusion that, in its expression, homosexual love does not differ from heterosexual love; its transport, tenderness, and passion are exactly the same. I repeat, *in its expression,* because, in depth psychology, a deep difference cannot be identified. Love permits us to escape our existential restrictions—explaining perhaps why writers often describe love in terms of light or illumination. Heterosexual love is a relationship *with the diverse.* Freud commented that woman remains a mystery; a woman psychologist might perhaps say the same of man. The heterosexual Eros offers us a view on a different area of experience; thus, by lighting up the other half of heaven, the world becomes more transparent. The union with something completely other than us implies that we, as half the symbol, can be recomposed only in the encounter with the opposite sex. By diversity, we intend here not only physical differences, but psychic as well; man and woman are psychologically complementary. All of this implies the natural extension of ourselves; from infancy, the male moves toward the female.

Why then, in the emotional and sentimental relationship, is the perception of the diverse so frightening as to motivate the homosexual option? The homosexual patient does not usually want to be cured of his homosexuality; he goes into analysis for some of the same reasons other patients do. If a common aspect exists, it is a result of the penalizing attitude of society toward those who stray from the dominant model. There is a growing tendency in certain psychoanalytical enclaves to listen more attentively to homosexual analysts in order to better comprehend their psychic world. This advanced attitude, however, is unfortunately still the exception, as the prevailing attitude in this area remains an exclusive one. However, I personally know two analysts—one Jungian and the other Freudian—who have had the courage to denounce that hypocrisy which exists in the psychoanalytical associations. I refer to the studies of Hopcke (1989) and Moor (1989).

Admitting the difficulty of providing exhaustive explanations on all the aspects of homosexuality, I personally believe that

119

motivating that particular compulsive choice is the psychological impossibility of approaching the diverse because it is seen as being too menacing. The female for man and the male for woman represent a challenge, whereas the similar or even the identical will obviously seem more accepting. In the man-woman relationship, the unconscious countersexual aspect can be projected outward so that the anima/animus become bridges leading to the other. This situation emerges in dreams, in which our unconscious heterosexuality can evolve through therapy. From a primitive state, it can evolve considerably, modifying even the type of partner attracting the individual. The anima and animus function like a lighthouse illuminating the other. A disturbed relationship with the animus or anima is inevitably reflected in the individual's unhealthy choices in life, one of the results of which is forming relationships in which she inevitably becomes bogged down in the same problem. In the male, as Jung commented, homosexuality can represent the condition in which he identifies with the anima, which results in his inability to project it outside. Thus, contrary to what usually occurs, he projects the persona coinciding with his own sexual identity. And it is here that a considerable diversity emerges between male and female homosexuality; the latter is apparently considered to be socially less alarming.

In male homosexuality, the genital dimension is one of the most important sustaining factors of the relationship, explaining the promiscuity of many homosexual men. What they go in search of is the sexual rather than the spiritual dimension. Jungian psychology identifies the archetypal foundation of this tendency in the great tradition of masculine genitalia, as expression of potency and vigor.

In female homosexuality, sexuality is far less important than friendship. In these very particular relationships, things like contact and participation have great importance. However, if we view this theme from the Jungian vantage point, the problem which eludes response is how, in that kind of relationship, completeness—or that unitary state of human existence which Jung himself indicated as the goal of the process of individuation—can be achieved (Hopcke 1989).

Fifteen

The Unpleasing Body

Qual fallo mai, qual si' nefando eccesso
Macchiommi anzi il natale, onde si' torvo
Il ciel mi fosse e di fortuna il volto?
[*What fault, what immeasurably iniquitous excess*
Sullied my very birth, causing heaven and destiny
to be so pitiless . . .]
—Leopardi, *Ultimo canto di Saffo*

In *Paedrus* (235 c), Socrates refers to Sappho as "the beautiful." That reference, however, is to the beauty of her lyrics.
Baudelaire described her as "more beautiful than Venus" (Baudelaire 1857), but the general opinion is that Sappho was actually
not physically beautiful. In any case, in one of her poems, Sappho describes herself as "small and dark," the same description
more or less found in papyrus documents dating back to the
second and third centuries (Campbell 1982). While there is no
way, obviously, to verify the exactness of that description, it is
interesting to learn that the legend of the ugliness of Sappho had
considerable support and was widely and variously expressed. It
is given credit, for example, in the poetry of both Ovid and
Leopardi. Ovid, in the *Heroides* (ep. XV), describes the poetess
writing to her lover Phaon, and Leopardi (1976, vol. 1) imagines
a "final canto" by Sappho. In both poems, Sappho laments her
own ugliness. In the letter Ovid imagines her writing to Phaon,
her very survival seems to hang on his acceptance of her love.
And, on a certain level, "The Last Canto of Sappho" can be read
as the tale of a suicide to which Sappho is driven by the realization of her own ugliness and Phaon's rejection.

An ugly body, therefore, could be perceived as existing on the confines of the obscure regions of death; it is a body condemned—for absolutely incomprehensible reasons—to extinction, to nonlife. The drama of the "ugly" Sappho, of certain poetic tradition and imagination, becomes perfectly comprehensible in the light of the Greek concept of beauty. That perception of the world (the Greek word for *world* being *cosmos*, that is, "beautiful and ordered world") associates beauty with measure and proportion, the Golden Mean, truth and good, Eros. If for the Christians, in their doctrine of *privatio boni*, as well as for the Greeks, evil corresponded to a sort of nonbeing—as well as in light of the close connection established in the Greek mind between goodness and beauty—we must assume that ugliness, and therefore the ugly body, were relegated to a nonbeing because they were perceived as dangerous within a world of proportion and beauty.

According to the religious scholar Angelo Brelich, the classical comedy of Aristophanes—in which the baseness and therefore the ridiculousness of existence unfolds—permitted the Greek spectator to experience, unharmed, one of the greatest dangers of existence, which was being below the Mean. The other danger—surpassing it—was the experience provided in the "shiver of tragedy" (Brelich, 1969, 117–118). The ugly, therefore, was excluded from the measure or the Mean, and for the Greeks that was equivalent to belonging to a realm which excluded life. If we consider that beauty for Plato and the neoplatonists was bound to Eros, to the point that it was considered an access to the absolute, we will understand the intense drama of the "ugly" Sappho. But how did Sappho rationalize her own ugliness? To what principle should ontological responsibility be attributed? The poets besides Sappho who considered the extreme nature of ugliness were not long in providing answers.

In Ovid's *Heroides* (XV, vv. 31–32 of the Latin text), for example, the poetess is imagined as having written, "envious Nature deprived me of beauty." *Envious* is the term used to correspond to *difficilis* (Leto 1966). Now, *difficilis* brings to mind the difficulty in relating to an "ugly body." Nature does not facilitate the approach of an "ugly body"; in fact, it is rejected. And yet, must we not speak of betrayal? For is it not Nature itself which gives birth to the ugly? Leopardi is expansive in the "Last Canto of Sappho," lending his own voice to the poetess:

Qual fallo mai, qual si' nefando eccesso
Macchiommi anzi il natale, onde si' torvo
Il ciel mi fosse e di fortuna il volto?
In che peccai bambina, allor che ignara
Di misfatto e' la vita, onde poi scemo
Di giovanezza, e disfiorato, al fuso
Dell'indomita Parca si volvesse
Il ferrigno mio stame?
[What fault, what immeasurably iniquitous excess
Sullied my very birth, causing heaven and destiny
To be so pitiless? In what did my sin consist, a
child still, unaware of misdeed, which then was the cause of this
unforgiving blow to the thread of my life?]

Despite the advent of Christianity between the time of Ovid and that of Leopardi—which would perhaps explain the references in the "Canto" to prenatal, or original sin—Leopardi's poetry can nevertheless be considered in the light of the same "difficult nature" referred to by Ovid. In this context, Sappho's lament becomes the lament of one who has discovered an abyss between herself and nature, a glacial indifference, even hostility; unmistakable signs of nature's betrayal. Ovid's difficult nature thus becomes Leopardi's "stepmother" nature, and in one of Leopardi's later reflections (*Zibaldone*, 11 April 1829), he describes that betrayal thus: nature, by virtue of the law of destruction and reproduction, and in order to conserve the actual state of the universe, is regularly and perpetually the persecutor and mortal enemy of all those individuals, of every type and species, to whom it gives life. That persecution begins the very moment it produces them. That being the necessary consequence of the existing order of things does not create a particularly edifying impression of the intellect of the creator of that order.

There are unmistakable Gnostic echoes in that observation. To whom, in fact, can we compare the author of the actual state of the universe if not the Gnostic Demiurge and author of an imperfect creation and creature?

The legend of Sappho's ugliness introduces a problem, the radical nature of which eminently lends itself to analysis in the context of our discourse on betrayal. What significance does betrayal assume when—objectively, or as a consequence of a perception in itself distorted—one is convinced of having to exist in an "ugly" body? Although fairly common, this problem is rarely approached clinically. And yet, the body is one of the principal stages on which are played the sequence of troubling events making up the individual perception of identity.

From our point of view, the objective nature of a physiognomy is not as relevant as the individual's own perception of it—which will unquestionably be the source both of the most intense suffering and the most profound gratification. A basic human desire is to be pleasing to oneself. In fact, self-esteem consists not only of a realistic and positive evaluation of our personality, but also a liking and acceptance our body, including all its defects and attractions. It is important that we be satisfied with our appearance, because our body is the shelter in which we pass our entire existence. The uninhabited body, unrecognized and unaccepted, implies the impossibility of embracing our own existence as something irreducibly personal. Such disconnection from one's body creates a continual push toward the precipice of nonbeing, the extreme consequence of which is suicide; at that point no space exists to contain or protect us, there is no shelter or refuge in which we feel deserving. Feelings of rejection and shame for our corporeity cause terrible psychic suffering, which is only inadequately expressed as the sensation of there being nowhere to rest.

The perception that we are physically inadequate causes not only shame, but also a certain sense of the absurd. We are constantly aware of an undercurrent of sadness which in social contact is easily transformed into shame and, inevitably, the absurd, the ridiculous. When we feel out of place we become absurd, hopelessly ill at ease, and certain that we constitute an element of disturbance in the physical harmony around us; while everything else conforms, relates, is part of a whole, we are deformed, disjointed, excluded from relation. An example of such alienation is Homer's description of Thersites as "the ugliest man ever to come under Ilium" (*Iliad*, II). In fact, in Thersites' experience, ugliness and ridicule, pain and resentment, converge. The more Thersites' ugliness, his feeling of being out of step with the world and the values of the Achaean warriors, feeds his resentment, the more he inspires hate in the hearts of those warriors. Thersites' feeling of alienation and being outside the Mean is the characteristic that introduces this personage in *The Iliad* (II.211–221):

> Now the rest had sat down, and were orderly in their places,
> but one man, Thersites of the endless speech, still scolded,
> who knew within his head many words, but disorderly;
> vain, and without decency, to quarrel with the princes
> with any word he thought might be amusing to the Argives.
> This was the ugliest man who came beneath Ilion.

When Odysseus, in order to cut short his insulting speech, strikes him with the scepter of Agamemnon, Thersites sheds a large tear, and the spectacle of his pain provokes the laughter of the Achaean heroes. Thersites' pain, in fact, is considered ridiculous, whereas the violence perpetrated against him is praised as the most praiseworthy among the thousand praiseworthy things done by Odysseus (ibid., II.265–275):

> So he spoke and dashed the sceptre against his back and
> shoulders, and he doubled over, and a round tear dropped from
>   him,
> and a bloody welt stood up between his shoulders under
> the golden sceptre's stroke, and he sat down again, frightened,
> in pain, and looking helplessly about wiped off the teardrops.
> Sorry though the men were they laughed over him happily,
> and thus they would speak to each other, each looking at the
>   man next him:
> "Come now: Odysseus has done excellent things by thousands,
> bringing forward good counsels and ordering armed encounters;
> but now this is far the best thing he ever has accomplished
> among the Argives, to keep this thrower of words, this braggart
>   out of assembly."

Thersites' pain is therefore as out of place as his ugliness.

Thus, despite the usual clichés as regards female obsession with physical "care-rejection," it would be a mistake to consider the solitude of this condition as exclusively feminine. Men can also suffer from serious "ugliness complexes," which might be better defined as disturbances in the perception of self and body. However, while the ridiculous is disharmonious and what is without meaning vulgar, only that which is without expression can be considered truly ugly. Feeling ugly is therefore actually an experience of the soul—the experience of the wandering Jew, homeless, with no mother to care for him, whose endless abandoning of places and individuals reveals rejection, the occult artisan of his destiny.

At this point, we might make a brief etymological digression: the original meaning of the Italian word *brutto* (ugly) was *sporco* (dirty). Its generally accepted, although doubtful, derivation is from the Latin *brutus*, which means "heavy, weighty, inert, massive." The etymon of the English word *ugly* belongs to the semantic sphere of *frightful*, that which frightens and terrifies because of its associations with pain, suffering, anxiety. The ugly person, therefore, experiences firsthand the monstrous aspects of life. The Shadow acts on the body, transforming it into the symbolic expression of rejection, and conversely, rejection acts on the body, electing it the bearer of evil, the Shadow.

But an ugly or spoiled body is not only the product of a self-destructive attitude, it is a constant provocation, menacing the "wholeness" of others, challenging repressed instinct and the defensive elements of the persona. In this sense, according to Freud, ugliness becomes unsettling, indefinite, and obscure, calling up the projection of unconscious contents; it is an anxiety-generating image inspiring defensive reaction, embarrassment, rapid glancing away. It provokes the phantasm of our own aggressiveness and causes the reemergence of negated, psyche-threatening aspects. Why, for example, in kindergartens are children who are ugly, overweight, or have some physical deformity persecuted and made fun of? This cannot be simply explained by saying that children are naturally cruel, or that they sadistically take revenge on that persecutor; for such behavior is the need to negate the very existence of that which threatens by annihilating it.

The ugly individual not only experiences his own Shadow, he is forced to incarnate the Shadow of others, because against his will or, as we will see, by virtue of some process of which he is ignorant, he provides the fertile ground for this type of projection. When we encounter a deformed person, we discreetly look away. That reaction, however, conceals an interior problem. Remember the elephant man (in the wonderful film of the same name) who, as he flees from his persecutors, reminds them that he also is a human being. If we examine that in an endopsychic context and trace the paranoid dynamic to interiorized figures around which the subject's identity was constructed, it is impossible not to ask to whom that "message" is really destined—as that is the most elementary element of recognition conceivable. The ugly individual releases the phantasm of worthlessness, alludes to an impossibility of existing in the world, and once more calls up the most devastating of betrayals, that which was experienced in the primary relationship.

The ugly body therefore represents a compulsive exhibition of love rejection. There are no more powerfully aggressive activations than those of a mother rejecting her own child. The child is unable to comprehend the arbitrariness of that attitude, with the result that fantasies of fault are activated to legitimate the mother's attitude. Olievenstein wrote, in his *Le Non-dit des Emotions* (1988), that the sense of injustice is the principal motor of the unsaid of the ugly individual. This kind of mother, instead of accepting and containing the child's aggressive impulses, diminishing their power and rendering them less terrifying, returns them to the child amplified, thus inhibiting any possibility of discharge to the exterior. This rejection does not constitute merely a judgment on the child's ugliness. It is something more; it is rejection by that arm which provided our most primitive containment, the first human gesture experienced. This is why the tale of the ugly duckling strikes such deep chords; the story of love rejection, of a small creature out of place, far away from his real mother and siblings. By means of an expedient of extremes, the tale is absolutely in tune with the intensity of that infantile pain. Because the "duckling" belongs to another species, it *cannot* be recognized. It is kicked, rejected, humiliated, and starved, and in its frozen solitude precociously experiences the winter of life. At the end of that trial, which is equivalent to psychological transformation, it discovers that it has become a magnificent swan.

TO LOVE, TO BETRAY

The conclusion of this story is one 'more confirmation of the theory that the condition of ugliness is related to early exile; the transformation of the duckling is in fact one with its acceptance by other swans. The extraordinary expressiveness of the tale lies in its schematism: the ugly duckling, who did not want to be born, is the last who becomes the first, the most beautiful, most elegant king of swans. It is a typical fantasy of redemption; in the psychological context, the more extreme the idealization is, the more the individual will become trapped in a distorted perception of her own inadequacy.

Of what, therefore, does the unconscious strategy of one imprisoned in an ugly body consist? Paradoxically—although absolutely congruous in a psychological context—the ugly individual is dominated by desire. While his unconscious universe is entirely subjugated by desire, the energies usually used in the search for the fulfillment of that desire are absorbed by its repression. Confronting oneself and others with a body made ugly can therefore be considered an expedient for withdrawing from one's own and others' desire, retiring early from the game; avoiding rejection by anticipating it. This mechanism can be defined, in terms of relational psychology, as a "self-fulfilling prophecy." Examples of this are bulimia and anorexia, which are in different ways manifestations of unconscious, self-inflicted destructiveness toward the body; the prophecy "I cannot be loved" is self-fulfilling in the confirmation of the rejection those disturbances arouse. With the bitter and syllogistic sagacity characteristic of his maxims, Francois de La Rochefoucauld (maxim no. 86) observed that "our suspicions justify the deceit of others." The sentiment expressed in the collection of poetry ascribed to Theognis cited above is analogous: cautious of my enemies, it is ultimately my friends who betray me.

We can now approach that particular phenomenon of "bodily ugliness" which is, paradoxically, perpetuated by the individual herself. Not infrequently, we meet men and women who, although literally obsessed by the idea of losing weight, cannot, because they lack the necessary confidence and energy. This situation demonstrates that a healthy relationship with our bodies is not acquired by willpower alone; the body is truly the mirror of the soul, and the discomforts of the soul necessitate consider-

128

ably more complex and deeper attention. It is possible that the body stores memories which the mind cannot; the repression of infantile traumas in the unconscious, for example, can also take the form of concealing in the body intolerable impressions of fear and indifference experienced as a child. Consequently, the inability to accept one's own body as it is, the aversion to parts of it considered unacceptable or, more drastically, the deliberately ruining of it with drugs, alcohol, or food abuse, could all be representations of those unconscious complexes that can be expressed in the body without risking unbearable conscious revelation of their meaning.

Manifested in the physical dimension is all relationship with desire—desire here meaning life energy. Think of the gratification derived from the pleasures of the senses and the survival function these have in our existence. Considering ourselves "ugly"—that is, unworthy—means being inhibited in the life processes; it means the inability of having relationships in which affection is expressed with the body. In these cases, the individual will often compensate for his physical, and subsequently emotional, alienation with compulsive intellectual activity. The result of this is that all the innocence, and at the same time terrible unpredictability, of existence of which the body is the faithful messenger is paralyzed and imprisoned in the structures of exclusively logical thought. Certain ascetic choices, for example, are paradigmatic expressions of this: all the individual's psychophysical energy is consumed in controlling and mortifying desire, with the result that the horizons of life become progressively narrower. Asceticism is therefore, according to Olievenstein (1988), "a sublime alibi for the fear of confrontation." The strategy of the ugly individual is perhaps less sublime, but it is equally effective. Although it is generally agreed that beauty can be a most formidable weapon, in certain circumstances ugliness can be equally so.

Sixteen

The Body Betrayed

And when the woman saw that the tree was good for food, and that it was pleasant to the eyes, and a tree to be desired to make one wise, she took of the fruit thereof, and did eat, and gave also unto her husband with her; and he did eat.

And the eyes of them both were opened, and they knew that they were naked; and they sewed fig leaves together, and made themselves aprons.

—Genesis, 3.6–7

The earliest and most undeniable proof of our finiteness and mortality is the perception of the body. The body prevents any attempt to transgress its limits, constantly crushing any illusions we might have of omnipotence. The process by which the child emerges from the primary symbiosis is the earliest experience of death. Infantile omnipotence is betrayed by the perception of the separateness of bodies and is equivalent to a negation of the desire for fusion and a loosening of the unconscious embrace. Our corporeal identity at that point becomes rupture, confrontation, regardless of the fact that that distance is both ontogenetically and phylogenetically necessary. This chapter's opening passage from Genesis describes the reaction of Eve after she has been induced by the Serpent to sin against divine injunction. Thus, the history of humankind began with the sudden awareness of the body. The renunciation by Adam and Eve of the omnipotence of the creatural condition becomes the knowledge of good and evil, which implies becoming aware of the body, sexuality, and—consequently—mortality. In the seventeenth century, Torquato Accetto, in his brief but incisive treatise entitled *Della dissimulazione onesta* (*Honest Dissimulation*, 1641), interprets that first opening of the eyes as emblematic of the fact that dissimulation is as ancient as the world itself:

> Since the first man opened his eyes, thus becoming aware of his nakedness, he attempted to hide himself also from the view of his Maker; thus the effort to conceal was born with the world itself and the first emergence of the fault, and many utilized dissimulation for this purpose . . .

Also in individual development, the processes of the structuring of the ego and the integration of the corporeal image are parallel. The history of the body and the corporeal experience are one with the history of Western philosophical thought which, since Plato, has made the body-soul dichotomy the foundation of its disjunctive logic, with the result that psyche and soma are inevitably considered as contrasting. Corresponding to the life and death, heaven and earth, good and evil, high and low, nature and spirit polarities, are values and nonvalues. The soul must be divested of all materiality if the intellectual contemplation of ideas is to be possible. Only by forgetting the body can the spirit, thus purged of sensual appetites, encounter Truth.

Think, for example, of the endless variations of the body-soul dichotomy which for so long obsessed the Middle Ages and which produced asceticism, contempt for the body and its subordination to the intellect, mortification of the flesh, and the condemnation of its pleasures. In his recent study, *Solitudo carnis* (1990), a history of the body in the Middle Ages, Vito Fumagalli—on the basis of positions assumed by the great Abbot Odon de Cluny—wrote that, according to the monks (and others as well), the realization of the individual's most profound and noble calling is denied, compromised by all that which the flesh signifies.

Men of sensation, observed de Cluny, making a few salient references to St. Paul, "will never succeed in truly penetrating matters of the spirit" (ibid.). Analogously, in his exegesis of the transgression of Adam and Eve, Philo of Alexandria equated Adam with spirit and Eve with the senses. Thus, it is the senses that betray. We might consider the problem of visions and nocturnal pollution—not uncommon in monasteries—in which the betrayal of the body was in many ways associated with the betrayal of dreams. Dreams sully, plunging the dreamer into sin. In the monastic view, pollution, voluntary or involuntary, is in any case a victory of the devil. Flesh betrayed is flesh consigned to solitude; flesh, too alive and uncontrollable, confuses the spirit and impedes one's spiritual aspirations with its urges and unpredictable outbursts. Therefore it must be repressed, dominated, purified (ibid.).

Thus, "there is no redemption for the flesh, only *mortification*, in the literary and original sense of the term, death" (ibid.).

With Descartes, the distinction between *res dogitans* and *res extensa* reduced the body to a mere extension of an incorporeal ego, the only repository of subjectivity. The ego, the center of consciousness, is *other than the body*, which continues to be charged with negative connotations. Ours is therefore a "betrayed" body in the etymological sense, because it is a body consigned, transported beyond the realm of subject, to the misery of objects with which we can at most establish a relationship which inevitably presupposes otherness. In common parlance, the body is generally described as something possessed; we "have" a body, not we "are" a body. While the intellect cannot proceed without the establishment of a reflective distance from objects, the body has remained first on the field.

Nevertheless, all that which lies outside our psychological dimension is nothingness. It is illusion to seek gratification in objects—even demoralizing, when the body is experienced in a utilitarian way, which results in a complete expropriating of its value. We describe the body in anatomical terms, and science explains it on the basis of psychophysical mechanisms. However, it is never referred to as a body that can fall ill, for example, as a result of feeling excluded from the world. When we consult a physician, she concerns herself with the pathology of the body, never its *existential* significance (which is always an expression of psychic significance and therefore a very important part of experience). No one considers what living *in* a tuberculate body or a body riddled with tumors implies; these aspects are repressed by medical pathology.

As Thomas Nagel wrote, there exists an affective quality of events, the internal significance of which is impossible to understand through physicalism; that is, deterministic schemas to redefine the reality of sentiment in terms of physical stimulus and neuron processes. Falcolini (1990) observed that scientific progress as regards the human body was made possible by the dichotomous view of the body-soul relationship; consequently, science de facto betrayed the body

> by imposing on it its own concept of "natural," "physiological," "normal," which does not take into account the specific nature of each individual.

There is no room in that approach for the subjective dimension, a dimension which phenomenology translates into the notion of the body experienced as animated and not an object among others—not a psychophysical entity, but the primary medium for our being in the world. The body in question is *our* body and, as such, cannot be ignored.

Inattention to one's own physicality is only one of the effects of the splitting we have effected, or been submitted to, between soul and body. We may naturally refuse to recognize ourselves in the thoughts of others because *they do not belong to us*, but no one would dream of denying that he recognized himself in his own thought. Why, then, are we unable to recognize ourselves *in our own bodies*, as though they did not represent us as we would have them? Are they not equally ours? Delving into the past, we can easily discover the logical sequence of significance and continuity in the evolution of our thought; however, it is considerably more difficult to reconstruct a history of our bodies. It is as though we become aware of our bodies only in the event of illness, when they present problems. If the sense of life lies elsewhere—in something transcending the body, in the immortality of the soul—then exiling the body would be equivalent to negating death itself, transforming it into a passing moment. But, like anything that is repressed, the body, death, illness, will assert themselves everywhere, secretly and obsessively, in every expression of our culture. Illness and old age become taboos. The body is tortured in the quest for a perfection that renders it equal to all others, just as death renders it equal to all others. The aged or diseased body is feared, as it calls up phantasms of the end, the body's decay, and its irremediably temporal nature.

In today's culture, the body has been deprived of its dimension of becoming. The ideal body is a young body, which is only apparently vital because it lacks history and static because it has been emptied of its truth. The body's truth consists of possessing a form that occupies a physical space and is modified over time. As it is in continuous relationship with the world, the body cannot avoid change, and every change, every mutation— like every season—has its value. Thus, depriving the body of the quality of becoming is equivalent to perverting its significance. And that "technological" operation of subtraction could legitimately be interpreted as one way of betraying the body, or, according to Falcolini (1990), of experiencing the body, not as link to life, but as an obstacle, or "the perception of the body as an obstacle to being-in-the-world."

Consequently, as a result of the great value bestowed on the young and inexperienced body, it is only logical that a good deal of the consumer economy should be occupied with the care of that body. Thus, the target of that market—the body— can "be nothing while at the same time possessing a great deal." But does that emphasis really correspond to the rediscovery or a profound belief in the value of the body? What is the psychological significance of that excessive care? Adhering to the prevailing imperative absorbs all that which is interior or psychic, in an exterior effort to render it unrecognizable and above all to succeed in manipulating it. What others encounter, in fact, is not our body, but its image, just as what we encounter are not other bodies, but their images. And we are slaves of those images.

Identity always has a somewhat dual aspect, since it implies a continuous interplay of integration and alienation, identification and differentiation. While we recognize our entirety in the mirror-reflected image, our attention is simultaneously outside, an appropriation/expropriation. The image is also simultaneously a reflection of our interior dimension and the exterior; the double, the body/house we inhabit which may seem familiar or extraneous to us, in which we move and eliminate or introduce objects that at some point are no longer things but affective associations. It is in this symbolic dimension that identity takes form.

In a patriarchal society, the corporeal dimension is entirely assimilated to the feminine. The woman inhabits the house, sees to physical needs, inhabits the lower spheres of the instinctual, making dependence her way of life and proximity to nature her sterling attribute. The untenable violence of this cultural operation is obvious, among other things, in the contradiction of the message emanated. The woman is expected to be slim and attractive, but at the same time produce children. Her body—the mythical cradle of the collective imagination—is exalted, but her physiology is also diseased corporeity, to be hidden or, at most, offered to the clinical eye of the physician. Resulting from this identification will be disturbances in the woman's self-esteem, very often expressed through "performances" of her body, in the form of obesity or anorexia. The latter of these has illustrious historical precedent in the mystical asceticism of Catholic saints from the Middle Ages on up to the last century. Even today, in cases of anorexia nervosa, it would seem that the body was deprived of its dimension of becoming, its history, or else that becoming and history were betrayed, submitted to a rigid, omnipotent spiritualization. In this context, Ganzerli and Sasso (1979) observed:

> Only if skeletal is the body experienced as belonging, only if refused by the other, as body-challenge, body-fetish, negation.

The body of someone with anorexia nervosa reveals repression of its humanity, a fervent desire for perfection, and a rejection of anything reminiscent of its mortal nature (ibid.).

The body, that ever-present interlocutor in the quest for our own identity, will often checkmate us, be unfaithful to us, betray us. Leopardi, in his sublime description of the suffering of one betrayed by his body who is consequently deprived of love, compares him with a starving man attending someone else's banquet with no hope of partaking. And here, analogies take form between themes of self-esteem, betrayal, and death, which might be better understood if we considered once more the problem of the "ugly" individual. That individual incessantly asks the other to confirm/refute her self-image; however, whatever the response, things unfortunately will remain as they are. She may then, feeling devalued and lacking self-esteem, project her own incapacity to accept herself onto the other, subsequently with the result that she will feel betrayed. Her request for compensation will be insatiable and—as she unconsciously refuses to offer herself as the object of love—she will also most likely be excluded from the other's love.

Seventeen

The Unwell Body

Such is the body: a combination of elements the order
of which is revealed as being conflicting.
                    —Serge Leclaire, *Demasquer le Real*

Why do we fall ill? Can betrayal cause physical illness?
Chiozza (1986, 67) responds to the first question as follows:

> Man becomes ill because he conceals from himself a story the
> meaning of which is unbearable to him. His illness is for the most
> part a symbolic response, an unconscious attempt to change that
> significance, or its conclusion—which is the same thing.

Perhaps the desire to camouflage nature's indifference and silence before the event we call life led to the creation of the fantasy of life as divine gift, of which we must prove ourselves worthy every day of our lives. Illness is the door through which
death enters our lives, a premature opening which brutally reveals, not only life's precariousness, but also the absolute irrele-
vance of our very presence in the world. Illness is in fact an excellent demonstration of the absurdity of the idea of divine
justice, as it irreparably reveals the limits of the mercy and love
of God, the *puntum dolens* from which we must in some way
find protection. Illness is a challenge and the definitive test of
the faith of those who proclaim themselves believers.

But, thanks to the myth of original sin—and not only the biblical version—illness is also inseparable from the idea of the expiation of sin. We are once more presented with the concept of
earthly existence as an expiation of sin, a divine scourge, the trials of Job—life essentially as the road to redemption. What

illness does, in fact, is cause the empty abyss to yawn before us, interrupting the flow of our existence. It is a timeless limbo, a suspended present, in which the need for deeper meaning becomes more intense, in which the arbitrary nature of pain, doubt, disorientation, is countered with the concept that evil is essential to the existence of good.

In Gesualdo Bufalino's *Diceria dell'untore* (*Rumors of the Plague Spreader*, 1981, 47), one of the personages, an ill and anxious priest, observes:

> Sin was invented by men in order to justify the pain of life and in order to provide a reason for our being punished.

The ill, therefore, are the spreaders of plagues, the contaminated who threaten to contaminate—not only in the sense that, by exhibiting their illness they induce others to avoid them, but in a deeper sense which is subsequently the theme of Bufalino's beautiful novel: illness induces its victims to pose extreme, radical questions as to the meaning of life, which is considered by those around them a far more serious threat than physical infection. The proximity of the ill with death is disquieting; it is a duel with death.

In equating illness to divine punishment, Christianity touches on a very profound psychological truth; falling ill is experienced, at least initially, as persecution. We feel attacked, victims of an invasion—but, as it is our bodies which are occupied, we are totally incapacitated. Illness becomes the embodiment of the enemy intent on exiling us to the confines of life and death.

The person afflicted is suspended in a time-nontime dimension, which reduces his life to the space of an abnormally amplified past. He is unjustly expropriated of his existential future, and there is nothing more annihilating for a human being. He becomes a hunter of memories, returning to the past like an abandoned lover, in a desperate attempt to feel still a part of life. The discovery that one is terminally ill makes it impossible not to reconsider all significance, which up to then had seemed obvious. When we are ill, we are absolutely alone.

The unwell person is perceived as frightening and all common support is withdrawn. It is at this point that those monastic orders exclusively dedicated to the care of the ill find their raison d'etre. Some relationships actually break up when one of the partners learns that the other is seriously ill. But then, if caring for the ill were a natural inclination instead of the result of special devotion or commitment, it would not have been elevated, as it has, to a kind of state of grace. Illness becomes an admonition; the afflicted individual becomes a physical reminder of a generalized potential danger. It is in this sense that the psychological configuration of those opting to care for the ill interests us.

We have said that Christianity expresses a psychological truth that emerges each time we fall ill. It is impossible to avoid experiencing guilt or seeing the sign of divine vengeance in painful events because at the basis of those reactions are old and very widespread beliefs. In the Old Testament, it was God who hurled down the plagues of Egypt, and in concepts that contemplate metempsychosis, the presence of an illness is the tribute or expiation proving past guilt. In the Book of Job, the prophet, uncomprehending of what befalls him, implores God to explain why he has been castigated. This feeling of being in the God's line of fire, so to speak, causes such an oppressive sense of guilt in the "victim" that she desperately seeks the solidarity of others. That solidarity is usually withheld because the projections solicited by the afflicted individual are perceived as too alarming. The afflicted body "exits from silence." The afflicted body aggressively asserts its presence—the same body we were once aware of only occasionally, when we were hungry, thirsty, or tired. The body that previously performed its functions discreetly, without attracting our attention, now bursts onto the scene like a mutinous rabble. The implicit pact, the unquestioned expectation, is that our bodies serve us. Psychologically, underlying this conviction is the assumption of the ego that it constitutes the entire personality or, at any event, controls the less-evolved aspects. What actually happens is that, at a certain point, the body ceases to respond and, consequently, challenges that unrealistic assumption. The perfect mechanism has broken down and, at that point, the myths of the elixir of eternal life, the philosopher's stone, and so forth, emerge to perpetuate the fantasy of endless youth.

Why do we feel it necessary to explain the affliction? To what psychic sphere can we attribute that feeling of guilt? It is probably the message every illness conveys to its victim. In some way, certainly unconscious, the individual in question has taken the enemy into himself, rather than searching for it outside himself, as is usually the case. The diseased organ—perhaps for the first time—presents us with the most devastating of persecutors; perhaps the progenitor of all persecutors, the one inside us. But the danger signal (falling ill), by means of which the body warns us, not only must not and cannot be ignored (I am reminded of the opening scene of a wonderful French film in which a physician, after he diagnoses a tumor, is slapped). It must be interpreted and considered at all levels, including all its implications.

Beware of considering illness an exclusively somatic problem, for it can also represent the occasion to shed light on our complicated relationship with our bodies. Just as we become aware of our bodies only when we experience discomfort, so do we discover consciousness only when the unconscious resorts to similarly extreme methods of communication. Remember that the language of the body is a primary, preverbal means of communication, which can exert an extremely coercive power over others, who are unable to ignore its message. In psychological terms, the somatization of illness is a consequence of lost contact with the pathogenic conflict, whose access to consciousness has been obstructed. The first question, and a very pertinent one, that an analyst should ask about the individual who falls ill is: What has occurred to cause the illness and what purpose, in the psychic context, does the illness serve? The body is an indicator of the psyche. However, its language must be reconverted, translated back into terms of unresolved psychic conflict. Psychosomatic illness intervenes when our psychological level is either not a sufficiently evolved one, or unable to express itself symbolically, attacking us at our weakest point; the body. And, strange as it may seem, illness is always an accusation.

It is by now generally accepted that a state of depression can affect the immune system, exposing the individual to infections to which she would normally be immune. Those who must carry out important tasks will always be selected from among those who are never ill, precisely because they possess a psychological constitution capable of resisting illness. Those who never fall ill are very evolved psychologically and thus are able to symbolically translate internal states without acting on them externally. The use of body language implies that the individual's capacity to face conflict is fairly primitive. And, at that point, illness accuses us—but at the same time it allows us to accuse others. The result of this is a self- and hetero-directed aggressiveness. When one member of a family falls ill, his condition becomes a tacit reproach to all the others. He becomes the carrier of the symptom, the one who has unconsciously taken upon himself the expression and, at the same time, the perpetuation of the family's pathological equilibrium. Our life is a parable with a logical conclusion; the tragic reality is that our bodies *must* sooner or later succumb to illness. This aspect of life is expressed in a certain genre of painting, depicting men reading as they hold a skull— symbolizing the dramatic impossibility of separating project from conclusion, or their inevitable simultaneous presence.

Eighteen

In Pursuit of Death

When God, stretching imploring arms to heaven,
Under sacred trees, as poets are wont to do,
Remained lost in sorrowful silence,
As He pondered His betrayal by thankless friends;
Turning to those who waited below
Assorted in ambitious dreams to become kings, wise
    men, or prophets . . .
But benumbed and prostrated by a slumber of beasts,
Began to shout: "No, God does not exist!"
They slept on. "Friends, did you not hear the tidings?"
My brow clashed against the eternal;
I, bleeding, racked, aggrieved, and for how long!
Brothers, you deceive yourselves: The abyss!
Hell and the abyss!
There is no god on the altar of my sacrifice . . .
"God does not exist! God is dead!" But they went on
    sleeping!

—Gerard de Nerval, "Chimere"

According to Seneca, imperial Rome's greatest exponent of Stoicism, we should thank the gods that no one can be forced to go on living against his will, because only thus does one have the chance to defeat inevitability. However, we might also keep in mind that at that time the concept of suicide as a heroic act and a demonstration of human liberty was widely accepted. That period's most famous suicides included those of Lycurgus, Socrates (although he for the most part condemned it in his *Phaedo*), Diogenes, Demosthenes, Cato, and, of course, Seneca

himself. Seneca claimed that philosophers who denied a person's right to take his or her own life, sustaining that the person
must await its natural termination, were in error. To Lucilius he
wrote, "it means not realizing that thus the way to liberty is obstructed" (Seneca, *Letters from a Stoic*) and that every person has
the right to judge for himself as regards self-inflicted violence,
provided that it is clear that the foulest sort of death is by far
preferable to the most exalted of servitude (ibid.).

Although in his *Nicomachean Ethics* Aristotle condemns suicide as an act of cowardice and a crime against the state, Greek
law never considered suicide a crime, either ethical or religious.
Homer condemns neither the suicide of Oedipus' mother and
wife, Jocasta, nor that of Ajax, just as Virgil does not condemn
the suicide of Queen Dido, when she realized that she had lost
Aeneas forever. Philosophers in general, and representatives of
the Hellenistic school of thought in particular (Cynic, Stoic, Epi-
curean), all condoned suicide. The maxim, *Mori licet cui vivere
non placet*, was rarely questioned. Western condemnation of suicide is clearly tied to the advent of Christianity. In any case, the
condemnation was pronounced tardily, albeit clearly, by Augustine in his *De civitate Dei*, becoming official in 533, with the Second Council of Orleans. After 563 and the Council of Barga, anyone who committed suicide was denied Christian burial.
Although the Pagan world accepted a person's decision to die,
even considering it a liberating gesture which practically raised
one to the level of gods, in Christendom it was considered a sin
without appeal, a violation of the Fifth Commandment and the
life instinct—in other words, the betrayal of the pact contracted
at birth with God, society, and oneself. During the Renaissance
there was a certain inversion of this tendency, and suicide was
viewed more tolerantly.

In *Biathanatos* (1603), by John Donne, the great metaphysical
poet and man of the church, the theme of suicide is approached
from the theological, philosophical, and juridical points of view,
including an analysis of the evolution of the various attitudes toward it, from classical antiquity on up to the end of the Renaissance. What is interesting in this work is not so much the fact
that Donne negates the absolute validity of the suicide-sin equation, as much as the arguments he uses to sustain his theory.

Donne was certainly not the first Christian writer to affirm that in certain cases suicide is not a mortal sin; however, he was the first to demonstrate this—as paradoxical as it may seem—using Christ as an example. If Christ chose to die, giving himself voluntarily to death—which was Donne's premise—then it was no longer possible to sustain the absolute validity of the suicide-sin equation. According to Donne, Christ did in fact commit suicide, the demonstration of which would be those passages from the Gospel where *give up the ghost* (*emisit spiritum*) is used in place of *died*, as well as some passages from the Gospel of John (10.15, ". . . and I lay down my life for the sheep," and 10.18, "No man taketh it from me, but I lay it down of myself").

No matter how absurd the arguments sustained by Donne to support his theory might seem, he believed that it was not the crucifixion which ended the life of Christ, but Christ himself. If we reflect now on the importance the figure of Christ has in our culture, Donne's arguments—apart from any intrinsic validity—cannot fail to astound us. The idea of the founding symbol of Christianity committing suicide cannot fail evoke the radical pervasiveness of betrayal because, in a sense, that act would be a radical, cosmic betrayal. Jorge Luis Borges, in a brief essay on the work of Donne, also hypothesized that, concealed behind the suicide of Christ, is an even more lethal idea (Borges 1960):

> Donne suggests that Christ died voluntarily, and that would imply that the elements and the earth, the generations of men, Egypt, Rome, Babylon and the realm of Judea were dredged up from nothingness to deal him death. Was then iron created for nails, thorns for that mocking crown, and blood and water for wounds? The baroque idea perceptible in Biathanatos was of a god who creates a universe in order to construct his own gallows.

And, as regards Philipp Mainlander, Borges wrote:

> He was, like myself, a passionate admirer of Schopenhauer. Under his influence (and perhaps that of the Gnostics), I believe we are fragments of a God, who at the dawn of time, avid of non-being, destroyed himself. The history of the universe is nothing more than the obscure agony of those fragments.

144

I might add that the history of the universe is also the history of an equally universal betrayal which is consummated in every aspect of our daily lives. How can we then relate to a god as conceived by Borges; a god heir to the hard and maleficent Gnostic Demiurge who gives life and in the very act of giving it, maliciously snatches it away? What is to be done then with the image of a god who commits suicide and with that gesture condemns us to the non-sense of life?

But let us leave the suicide of God and return to life. The subject of suicide may appear extraneous to the theme of this book and, in fact, we have until now considered betrayal not only as inevitable in human affairs, but as a basic and *vital* element of our very existence. Admittedly, defining the act of taking one's life as "vital" might cause perplexity, but then we cannot ignore the extreme ambiguity of the word *betrayal*, not only in the etymological sense, but also *semantically*. As we now know, it was that ambiguity which makes possible the assertion that it is possible to betray without betraying; that is, breaking a pact, but in the name of a higher or deeper loyalty; betrayal as transgression, but on a level of that of Adam and Prometheus; a blessed and decisive sin, a *felix culpa*, a transgression essential to the human emancipation from Eden and the beginning of history. The concept of betrayal must be based on a pact, a promise. And the pact or promise par excellence is, beyond the shadow of a doubt, love. Our relationship with life is also one of love—from whence the expression "the love of life." But what role would suicide play in that relationship?

As we have seen, it is an implicit rule of our particular culture that death be camouflaged. The dream of omnipotence nourished by a technological society is already sufficiently challenged by every bodily defeat, illness, old age—in short, all that which might induce one to reflect on the precariousness and, consequently, the *sense* of existence. In this search for meaning— which is subsequent to no longer recognizing ourselves in those collective canons offering everlasting, ready-made existential meaning extraneous to our true individual values—death can be the occasion, perhaps the only one, to *choose* life. As long as we are prevented from choosing death—symbolically or, occasionally, even literally—we obviously cannot choose life. The existence of suicide implies that we *can* choose death.

All those who, by heeding the voice of their own interior dimension, come into conflict with the dictates of external convention, are responding to something that will inevitably bring them face to face with death. The courage to reflect on the sense of life and individual choice, in fact, involves reconsidering our imagined omnipotence, which implies the capacity to contemplate the inevitability of death. Only when we perceive, at a deep emotional level, the brevity of our appearance on earth will space be created for reflecting on the sense of life. Otherwise, we will remain as currents flowing passively downstream, secure in the illusion that our possessions, homes, professions, respectability, and descendance endow us with solidity and permanence, oblivious to the fact that all these identifications are a fossilization of our thought. And, all the while, the river of life will carry us nearer and nearer the unknown sea, which is death.

When some inner urge forces us to reflect on our lives— something which can happen during analysis, but also as a result of some violent event—that faith in materialism falters. It will no longer be enough simply to be so and so, to belong to a particular social class or family, or to practice a particular profession. The sudden, urgent need will arise for a newer faith to restore real significance. The results of the process activated by that urgent need for individuation are not predictable. An individual can be strengthened, becoming a happier human being, but she can also become lost forever in a labyrinth of bitter solitude. The danger involved in the quest for meaning should not surprise us since—as Jung observed—acquiring consciousness is tantamount to stealing the sacred fire of the gods, a Promethean sin. And, as it involves coming into contact with the unconscious dimension, it requires the courage to put aside everything that was familiar to us before the numinous entered our experience. Moreover, there is no guarantee that the ego will be up to the test. It is not our intention here to have the last word on individual destiny. Suicide is usually considered the dramatic result of a conflict between worldly and interior laws impossible to resolve in a way acceptable to the individual. But who can say whether, for certain individuals, suicide is not the action which liberates?

The position of David Hume in his work, *On Suicide*, is in some ways in line with our discourse. Suppose, Hume says, that I no longer have the capacity to promote public interest, that in short I constitute an obstacle, or that my life prevents another from being useful to the community. In that case, taking my own life would not only be blameless, it would actually be praiseworthy (Hume 1756). He also states that it is impossible to negate that suicide can in certain circumstances be considered a "duty towards ourselves" (ibid.). The circumstances Hume refers to are illness, old age, or any other unpleasant event that renders life unbearable. Jung expressed a similar opinion in a letter to Eleanore Bertine on July 25, 1946. In certain cases, he wrote, suicide can be in harmony with the unconscious of the person committing it, and at that point, preventing it would be absolutely illegitimate, almost a crime.

Every betrayal is experienced as an injustice, but the feeling of injustice at having been betrayed in our expectations by life itself—which appeared to offer us its fruits and then cruelly denied us the means to gather them—is intolerable. That experience could be compared to the cruel Sphinx, who poses endless riddles to her children. Yet, according to Camus (1942), judging whether life is worth living is equivalent to solving a basic philosophical mystery. All the rest—whether the world is three-dimensional, or whether there are nine or twelve categories of souls—is secondary, only games. The answer comes first.

We must first find a response to the question of meaning and, paradoxically, the decision to die can constitute one response. Volunteering to go to war or going on a hunger strike for an ideal could be considered transverse forms of suicide. Camus is enlightening when he says that what is called a reason for living is at the same time an excellent reason for dying (ibid.).

Turning this affirmation around, we could say that at times a reason to die only reinforces the will to live. It might then be possible that the fatal and definitive act of suicide conceals, with the accusal of life's betrayal, a magisterial request to have unveiled what life denies us. Suicide betrays life, reveals its wealth experienced as unattainable. The double aspect of the gesture—both its obvious destructiveness and its potential as a desperate and autarchic bid for redemption from nonauthenticity—is illustrated also by the frequency of suicide notes. In these, there is still space for the world, a final attempt to communicate with it, and above all—given that in most cases the message explains the act—also the request that the act be given attention, interpreted, perhaps even understood.

Schopenhauer sustained that the person who commits suicide actually desires life, and in fact the tragically exuberant thirst for life revealed by some famous persons who committed suicide is astonishing. The American poet Sylvia Plath was one example. In a letter to her mother, she described her ". . . paradoxical joy of . . . being and intense sense of living more richly and deeply in the world than any other" (Plath 1975). But she was equally conscious of the "roots of sorrow and hurt" (ibid.) from which that joy flowed. In her poem "Ariel," Plath wrote:

> And now I
> Foam to wheat, a glitter of seas.
> The child's cry
> Melts in the wall.
> And I
> Am the arrow,
> The dew that flies
> Suicidal, at one with the drive
> Into the red
> Eye, the caldron of morning.

Another great writer, the Japanese Yukio Mishima, who committed suicide on November 25, 1970, left an astounding message (Yourcenar 1980):

> Human life is brief, but I would live forever.

Far from labeling the decision to die either as necessarily pathological or necessarily healthy, we will limit ourselves to considering the possible meanings of suicide, which is no less a reflection on the meaning of life. I am convinced that if there were more permissiveness as regards psychological crisis there would be less recourse to suicide as the only escape from unbearable solitude. As long as the surrounding world remains rigid and obstinate in its negation of the reality of suffering, the suffering individual will remain trapped in unbearable solitude and alienation. Suicide concerns us all, not only because that gesture in others, even if only remotely, has touched all of us at some point in our lives, but also because the *thought* of our own suicide cannot have failed to cross our minds, even if fleetingly, as a radical reaction to intolerable frustration, mourning, separation, defeat. As Jean Amery wrote in *Hand an sich legen. Diskurs uber den Freitod* (Committing Suicide, 1976), the threatening dimension of that *echec*—more obviously than death itself—subtends every human existence.

The causes of so desperate a reaction can be as varied as the solutions eventually found for that desperation. However, we might at this point attempt to shed some light on the deep motivations leading to the decision to put an end to an existence.

There is a famous observation of Freud's, a reflection which has always been particularly comforting to me in difficult moments (Freud 1929):

> Life, as we find it, is too hard for us; it brings us too many pains, disappointments and impossible tasks.

While that observation might appear to be the result of an extreme pessimism, it could also be the observation of someone who had *really lived*.

At the beginning, life was full of promise: when we were thirsty, someone gave us something to drink; when we were hungry, someone fed us; when we were tired, someone rocked us to sleep. At that point in life, faith in the *justice* of the external world is total, because our demands are constantly satisfied, and a life which so promptly recognizes our rights causes us to feel just. It is this sense of justice that leads us to make an unconscious, iron pact with life (which we are sure will always be on our side). Up to then, all we desired, all satisfaction of our needs, seemed within reach. The sensation that life is beautiful is constantly reinforced by our experiencing only immediate gratification.

As we grow, however, the first difficulties, the first frustrations, the first unsatisfied requests, begin to take form. Our sense of justice begins to weaken and eventually completely disappears.

At this point, the unconscious pact between the individual and life suffers the first blow. We can never stress sufficiently the fact that justice is always perceived as something objective, absolute, universal, and impartial.

Consequently, with the passing years, we inevitably end up trusting only in divine justice, having reached the conclusion that human justice simply does not exist. We grow up with the idea of justice as an element ruling the world, somewhat like Newton's gravity. However, as we have seen, life's true countenance is soon enough revealed as being indifferent, beautiful, cruel, at times compassionate (albeit always fortuitously so), incongruous, and chaotic. And not even a shadow of a certitude remains; in other words, life is not to be trusted. The initial pact is painfully broken, and the betrayal of life as a result of the violation of that pact brings to mind Leopardi's tragic verses ("To Silvia"):

> O Nature, O Nature,
> Why do you not deliver
> that which you promise? Why do you deceive
> your children of so much?

It is life, then, that betrays us; life which—if we return to the original meaning of *to betray*—consigns us to the enemy, to death. Death is meant here, however, not as a natural death, which is inevitable although all the same often unexpected, because we are consigned to that one from birth. It is another death, one meditated upon and decided on, at times after lengthy and meticulous preparation—suicide.

There is no way of knowing whether those suicides apparently the result of sudden impulse were in fact spontaneous or premeditated. In all probability, they had been considered for some time in situations in which the continuous presence of betrayal had become unbearable. And here we must consider once more the various meanings of *to betray*. Besides "to consign," it also can mean "to unveil." In what way does life's betrayal unveil something by not maintaining the illusions of our childhood? Life's betrayal unveils the presence of the soul. Consequently, from the psychological perspective, suicide can only be approached from the point of view of the soul. It is only before the potential of suicide that we become aware of our own psychic life, of the fact that we possess a soul, just as we discover our own individuality through experiencing the possibility of suicide. Individuality implies the courage to rise up alone against a world that betrays and renders banal. And it is from thence that the deep desire to leave that world springs.

We must not forget that the word *courage* has been used in the discussion of suicide since classical times. Taking responsibility for ourselves in an autonomous and critical way, in fact, is an act of reappropriation requiring a certain separation from the past. For that reason, analysis often implies experiencing a kind of suicide or taking of our lives in order to transform and allow new life to emerge through the abandoning of the old, moribund model. In the symbolic language of the psyche, however, abandonment is equivalent to death. As long as life proceeds without any great upheavals, with gratifications which are real or illusory, the soul can be considered as being eclipsed, set aside, reduced to silence. Unfortunately, not only is this condition precarious—as the underlying equilibrium between desire and satisfaction is precarious—but the deprivation of the soul is a losing proposition in itself. Denying the presence of our soul implies renouncing a precious gift, because the soul is also our strength. Most individuals, however, either do not even suspect the existence of the soul or consider it part of moral, political, or religious allocution. The soul exists to the extent that it has been institutionalized by those whose profession it is to believe in it.

Suicide causes perplexity. Its occurrence inevitably creates general stupor and a widespread feeling of guilt, as if in some way everyone were responsible for it. Jung, in a letter of July 10, 1946, expressed the suspicion that, in the final analysis, the effort to live is in itself important, and that the purpose of our lives is to achieve the highest possible level of spiritual development and a heightening of our consciousness. Our lives, our energies, must all be directed towards reaching that goal (Jaffé 1975, 68).

Life, according to Jung, is an experiment that must be completed. However, choosing to die remains a possible alternative, as well as represents the extreme response to life's betrayal.

Nineteen

Death Encountered

Oh, multiplied misery! We die, and cannot enjoy death.
—Donne,
"Devotions upon Emergent Occasions," 1. *Meditation*

The urge toward suicide is more than just a destructive drive, a "thrombosis of the soul," or the "savage god" referred to by Alvarez (1970). It is, paradoxically, a coded message of sorts, revealing to us a radically different—even contrasting—reality, and consequently *the desire for new life*. It constitutes a very delicate moment, and at that point we must discover for ourselves whether life has really consigned us to death or is instead indicating to us a painful itinerary leading to the discovery of the soul demanding commitment of the deepest kind. Etty Hillesum (1981) observed that at times life is difficult and terribly discouraging, when we are agitated, troubled, and tired at the same time . . . when we can do no more than lie still under the blankets, waiting patiently for that discouragement and desperation to pass. "Once I reacted foolishly in that state; I began to drink with friends or considered suicide or read from a hundred different books for the entire night."

What is that pressing urge, that desire to say no to a life which cruelly disappoints us, shattering our dreams? What really dashes our projects and dreams, bringing us rudely back down to earth, are our relationships—the source of maximum suffering and minimum happiness. Relationship is the ambience par excellence of continuous transformation, in an everlasting alternating of roles, from wounded to healed to wounded.

In *Symbols of Transformation*, Jung considers the initiation to individuation as symbolic of death and resurrection. We have seen how individuality implies betrayal. We have also seen how the phase of "forbidden incest" is equivalent to a symbolic phase to overcome the hidden plot, the omnipotent and endlessly enthralling mother-son dyad. The neurotic incapacity to detach from the mother reveals a fear of facing the initiatory passage from one stage of existence to another, more conscious world of suffering. Murray Bowen wrote that the lower the level of differentiation is, the stronger the unresolved emotional attachment is to the parents (Bowen 1971–1972). In this case, what comes into play is a radical, powerful aversion to the process leading to heightened consciousness. That aversion—which is equivalent to betrayal—here intended in the etymological sense of condemning the potential of the anima to the condition of nondifferentiation—could in fact be the result of a terror of that initiatory process leading to another kind of existence, a passage which could seem equivalent to death. It was that process the alchemists referred to when they spoke of *distractio* or "voluntary death."

Otherwise, why would we fail to recognize our own projections, and why do the lives of so many drag on in that state of nonrecognition which is betrayal of the animus? In *The Psychology of the Transference* (1946, 262), Jung wrote:

> the merely natural man must die in part during his own lifetime.

The merely natural person must be transformed into the spiritual person and, according to Jung, the Christian symbol of the cross is still the most exemplary and valid expression of that transformation. That passage was expressed by the alchemists as death; in other words, a temporary suspension of the psychic life. In this sense, there is also a perceptible unmasking of projections characterizing the merely natural individual— an experience so agonizingly painful as to explain that "aversion everybody feels when he has to see through his projections and recognize the nature of his anima" (Jung 1955–1956).

That thesis can also be reversed, in which case "real death" can at times be considered the consequence of one's rejection of knowledge of the Self. In this context, Jung (ibid.) wrote:

153

> If the demand for self-knowledge is willed by fate and is refused, this negative attitude may end in real death.

Consequently, choosing growth also implies choosing death; symbolic suicide. And, like it or not, it also implies killing, killing oneself. Similarly, through fantasies of suicide, a tendency may begin in the conscious mind toward that transformation rendered urgent by the soul's suffering. The rebel Isai, the protagonist of *Mishima's Horses in Liberty* (Yourcenar), commits suicide after failing a terrorist coup, that suicide he had so often fantasized as a sublime instant, "seated under a pine tree, on the coast, at sunrise." The defeat of the desire for social transformation is another expression of the failure to transform, and the act of suicide its inevitable epilogue. On another level, van Gogh also failed, in the artistic parable, to symbolically effect a transmutation of that ego which his blazing, solar colors projected onto the canvas.

Betrayal and suicide share the same literal ambiguity, which can ensnare anyone failing to view the reality of existence symbolically or transcending facts in order to be open to an initiatory and redeeming death. The Italian press not long ago reported on what appeared to be an epidemic of suicides involving a number of northern Italian towns. Those suicides, committed by little more than adolescents, were a response to the failure to shake off a subtle and invisible *mal de vivre*, unrecognizable to most.

"The only horror is not to be used," wrote Marguerite Yourcenar in *Fires* (1957, 33). Not being used for anything or by anyone implies existing as a mirror incapable of reflecting. The world withholds acknowledgement, and the key to reality and our being in the world remains inaccessible. We ask the world to restitute our image, which—because of some mysterious plot originating at the dawn of existence—is dissipated in the abysmal black holes of daily life. We could say that the dream pursued in life is spoiled through the incessant request for mirroring, reflection, and, consequently, recognition.

The concept of suicide alludes to transformation; however, the more radical the prospective change is, the stronger the impression of *danger* will be. Acting on the suicidal impulse may also

154

seem the best way to resolve conflict. At this point life betrays us by consigning us to death. But, paradoxically, we also are the perpetrators of betrayal, because the impulse to kill ourselves does not necessarily mean the act itself so much as understanding its significance. Therefore, if we fail to grasp the sense of the impulse, we will—like inept translators— misinterpret the sense of the word, consequently betraying the intention.

The idea that suicide and death constitute the first perturbation of the soul has always been a theological assumption. Consequently, death can represent the *figure through which the soul speaks to us*. As the emergence of individuality may be considered partially the result of an awareness of the possibility of suicide—and consequently, choosing life over death—then, in the process of becoming ourselves, we begin constructing our "ship of death."

As the philosophers would have it, going consciously toward death means constructing the best vessel possible. Also according to Plato, being a philosopher was equivalent to preparing for death. The skeptical Montaigne was of the same opinion. Jung wrote in his autobiography that, if consciousness really continues after death, that continuation can only be conceived of as psychic. Also according to Jung, such continuation implies that life beyond death could only be represented "as moving through the world of images." Therefore, it is the soul which goes to dwell in the world beyond, in the land of death. Thus, if "unconscious" and "land of death" appear to indicate the possibility of homologous horizons of meaning, the recognition and accompaniment of images that take form in life prepare us for death and the passage beyond (Jung 1961). Jung in this way, by transvaluating the lesson of Plato, reclaims it. Carrying this idea to the extreme conclusion, we could say that everyone—albeit unconsciously—chooses his own way of meeting death. The choice of method will only be more or less evident.

The failure of the existential project, which alone confers meaning to our present, can lead to suicide. As long as we are oriented toward the future and there is no obstacle to our growth, as long as there is this ray of light illuminating the way, maintaining the impression of continuous expansion, the idea of suicide will not occur to us. It will occur, however, the moment we become aware that the possibility of growth no longer exists. The project represents the subjective horizon of meaning, in which we include present events, on which the vitality of our dimension of desire above all depends. The project with which we identify can be of the highest spiritual or the most material nature. However, the project's specific nature is not important, because the "within" and "without" can at times coincide. For example, career possibilities in adult life translate this desire into the future projection of the present. Through that projection, the individual feels part of a process, carried along, literally "on the move."

Nazi concentration camps have often been the subject of psychological studies, as the camps represent real situations of confines, extreme limits of survival. There, suicide was explicitly and *strengstens verboten* (strictly forbidden). The Nazis were only too aware of the fact that that prohibition represented the definitive expropriation of the prisoner's identity. In this context, those prisoners who deliberately threw themselves against the high-tension barbed wire fences were remarkable. Unquestionably, that act was an attempt to end unbearable suffering, but it was also their only remaining possibility to assert their ego.

The temptation to commit suicide becomes irresistible when we realize the absolutely gratuitous nature of our pain, when it appears without any meaning whatsoever. Torture is bearable if, with our silence, we can save the life of a friend, a loved one, and so on. It becomes totally unbearable when it is pointless. Suicide can be the result, for example, of an unbearable absence, mourning, or separation. The absence of a relationship with our interior world can result in our sense of individuality being delegated to another, to an extent well beyond anything to be reasonably expected from a relationship. In similar cases, psychological assistance, even unprofessional—a friend or (for believers) a priest—can be of great comfort. The strength of the person with a faith lies in her concept of the world, a concept that includes no dangerous voids. All religious systems, as we have seen, originated as a response to fundamental questions of human existence. In fact, the development of the religious dimension could be seen as part of a process of evolution prolonging survival.

Suffering leading to suicide can therefore be the result of the soul's awakening and the urgent need for meaning that it creates. As I mentioned above, the idea, or the actual act of suicide, is never sudden, but the culmination of an inner process which is often secret. Fantasies of suicide are signs of a desire for that richer reality and existence which nature, after having promised so much, cruelly withheld. Every betrayal is experienced as injustice, but *this* injustice is truly unbearable—so unbearable as to create in those experiencing it the paradoxical, if assuaging, necessity to feel deserving of it, so as to justify it. It is the same irresistible drive—so irrational but at the same time so eminently rational—to find ethical justification for everything, from natural catastrophe to the Biblical plagues. It was in this sense that Voltaire, in *Candide*, criticized Leibniz's theory that humanity inhabits the best of all possible worlds, railing against that extreme optimism which found justification for everything, including the catastrophic Lisbon earthquake. Consequently, we end up accepting the idea that, for sins unknown to us, we deserve even that betrayal.

It is necessary to understand the relationship with reality of the person contemplating suicide, as well as what sort of life it was that he desired and was denied. In his memoirs (1961), Jung describes his difficult search for the meaning of life, relating the darkest moments of that trial to the failure to understand dreams. A voice inside him said: "You *must* understand the dream, and at once!" That voice became progressively insistent and ferocious, to the point of thundering, "If you do not understand the dream, you must shoot yourself!"

It is not difficult to imagine how suicide might seem an inviting prospect—a way out, a solution—at times when we feel paralyzed before some task, suddenly handicapped, unable to flee or defend ourselves. Life besets us mercilessly, after having deprived us of our capacity to face it. This is nature's great betrayal. We could say then that we are betrayed by life when it denies us perspective. With no prospects, we might just as well have already committed suicide. Consider the desperation caused not only by the inability to feel confident and present in the affective sphere, in the more or less important events of our everyday lives, but also incapable of any optimistic anticipation for something that *might* be acquired.

It is the desperate heart which invokes death, the desperate soul which deals itself death. When one of my patients discovered that he had contracted AIDS, as a psychoanalyst I was faced with an enormous problem, because the person before me (young, as opposed to most individuals suffering, for example, from tumors) had been condemned to death just as life was beginning, when life was still before him. It was as if the fantasy of his own death permitted transformation—although in a hallucinatory form. In this context, suicide only means: "I do not accept the fact that a life still entirely to be lived should end. To this betrayal of life, I can at least counter my own desperate will."

The idea of death necessarily presupposes an elaboration, a taking distance from the past. If this idea is not metabolized, it will annihilate us, crush us with its weight, which will be in proportion to the degree of unproductiveness. The impression is one of having saved old and useless objects, which little by little have occupied the entire space, leaving none for anything new. Suicide is the last *ratio* we have, if we have never had the courage to metabolize the past in order to look to the future instead of going back to what we could or should have done.

Our mental health necessarily lies in being able to prevent the past from annihilating us. We have two alternatives: to live or to die. And the choice must be made in perfect solitude. Metabolizing the past means constantly accepting the prospect of death; for example, we must be capable of abandoning the love experience, if that is the condition to our being open to what is new. The creative force must destroy in order to produce something new. Birth requires a future freed from the past. We can become desperate, convinced that we are no longer alive, causing a somatization of that condition of deprivation. The idea of suicide in moments of physical suffering becomes dominant because that suffering compounds the negation of our development. Here, the idea of betrayal has become physical, concrete—at which point, suicide seems the only way out. It is difficult to present this act as symbolic. In these situations, only religious convictions may predominate because, when there is no hope and nothing seems to have any meaning, the soul—which is "naturally religious"—senses the presence of God.

Dying constitutes a daily challenge in the same way that cells continuously regenerate by dying. We might even say that anyone to whom the idea of suicide has never occurred has never courageously taken stock of her own life or embraced the idea of transformation. The response to the desire to commit suicide lies in listening to the voice of one's soul. That voice speaks when the gratifications of life disappear and the true, cruel countenance of nature is finally revealed. Nature's cruelty would "consign" us to death, and suicide is what seals that betrayal. However, at this point, there is also the danger of failing to "unveil" the sense of our gesture, by negating a voice to the event of inner transformation which our suicide must not suffocate, but reinforce.

Twenty

Death Desired

In nothing more than death must we follow our soul's disposition.
— Seneca, *Letters to Lucilius*

Death is the ultimate betrayal and, therefore, "the analyst cannot proceed without a philosophy of death" (Hillman 1964); if he did, he would betray the other as well as himself. And yet, death resists all deciphering; it is the "non-abode" of experience or, as Baudrillard put it, the abode of "irremediable deviance." Mourning the death of another, considering our own death through grief, illness, pain, vulnerability, the perception of the inexorably diminishing of our vital forces, the solitude and pain of real or imaginary failure—whatever the reason, the discourse on death and dying becomes rarefied, refractory, finally retreating into silence. The horizons limiting the human dimension cause the shadow of death to be cast over all we do or desire.

Never before in the course of human history has there been so desperate an attempt to exorcise the fear, even the idea, of death through the myth of progress, overproduction, but above all, through the hysterical use of time, as though death's distressing image and dark message could be eliminated in that astonishing vortex. But attempting to "betray" death, to eliminate its presence or destroy its power with modern rites, has only succeeded in fearfully magnifying its shadow. And, while modern elixirs of long life and techniques for aesthetic perfection proliferate, creating the illusion of timelessness, we have all been exposed indiscriminately to the possibility of sudden and total atomic destruction.

The truth is that we cannot betray death without betraying our-selves, and not only because of its continuous presence, with the loss of those dear to us, the loss of love or the advent of illness, which beats out the rhythm of our psychic time, but because the idea of death implies that our existence will not be fulfilled—which implies a void, an absence of meaning for our being in the world. Thus, death and betrayal aid and abet each other, and in this sense an interpretative and less literary approach to Christian theology and its symbolism reveals the true triumph of death as being not only its power to destroy what is material, but also its capacity to annihilate individual vocation; in other words, all ex-istential projects. The victory of death filters into the present when we fail to master it with our awareness—when it guides our steps, as Emily Dickinson wrote (*Poetry*, vol. 2):

Through all its former places, we
Like individuals go
Who something lost, the seeking for
Is all that's left them, now.

Betraying ourselves implies the death of the soul. And depres-sion, with its sad corollaries, is a living death—or better still, the perception of death only as annulment, disintegration, radical loss of meaning, the darkness in which we drown. Depressed individuals, in fact, often describe their condition as "being dead." That very language, as Kristeva (1987) commented, ex-presses the loss of all meaning, the realization of insignificance, emptiness, the void: "melancholy man is estranged from his own language."

The infinite possibilities of being human also include counter-ing difficulty and discomfort with betrayal and consigning one-self to a long, lucid, and tedious night. It is not my intention to pass moral judgment on the individual's choice of life or death; we are too familiar with the complexity of the soul to confine it in the narrow limits of opinion. However, the decision to be-come analysts—in itself the incarnation and demonstration of a passion for the suffering voices of the soul—sustains an unfail-ing faith in the regenerating potential of the psyche. It is in a sense the declaration that we dare to accept, to risk, challenge.

For, if we fail to accept life's challenge, a greater failure will not be long in arriving, for an unlived existence is infinite betrayal. Apropos of this is Edgar Lee Masters' *Spoon River Anthology* (1914), that poetic collection of portraits, in the form of brief communications of the dead, who provide impressionistic sketches—through memories, youthful events, remorse, and regrets—of their "betrayed" destinies. Of those portraits of individuals, either misunderstood or themselves incapable of understanding life, the portrait of George Gray is of particular relevance:

> I have studied many times
> The marble which was chiseled for me—
> A boat with a furled sail at rest in a harbor.
> In truth it pictures not my destination
> But my life.
> For love was offered me and I shrank from its
> disillusionment;
> Sorrow knocked at my door, but I was afraid;
> Ambition called to me, but I dreaded the chances.
> Yet all the while I hungered for meaning in my life.
> And now I know that we must lift the sail
> And catch the winds of destiny
> Wherever they drive the boat.
> To put meaning in one's life may end in madness,
> But life without meaning is the torture
> Of restlessness and vague desire—
> It is a boat longing for the sea and yet afraid.

In her autobiographical works, Simone de Beauvoir often recalls the overwhelmingly negative effect paternal betrayal had on her adolescence. Profoundly disappointed by life and in disastrous economic conditions, her father vented his frustration on her, pointing out her clumsiness and presumed ugliness, causing her to feel in conflict with herself and others. She recalls that, at that age when young girls dream of their woman's bodies and first love, her father would often say, "Simone is a man!" It is not difficult to imagine the possible effect of this on an adolescent's most intimate and feminine needs. Simone de Beauvoir herself lists the long series of symptoms, psychosomatic disturbances, real phobias, and tics which constellated that critical period. She abandoned herself to reverie and fantasy to compensate for the oppressiveness of the present. In fact, it was during that period that her vocation as a writer emerged clearly as a means of deliverance and emancipation from her condition. Later on, in *Pour une morale de l'ambiguité,* at an age when it had finally become possible for her to probe the past and see its betrayals as the dark road to a predestined growth, she wrote that it was only because of the existence of real dangers, failures, and earthly damnation that the words *victory, wisdom,* and *joy* have meaning (Francis and Goutier 1985).

Every experience associated with painful events implies crisis and the contraction of the individual's vital space; discourse reduced to silence, weeping, and illness. M. Yourcenar, in *Memoirs of Hadrian* (1951), wrote:

> Meditation upon death does not teach one how to die; it does not make the departure more easy, but ease is no longer what I seek . . . It is conceivable, after all, . . . that death is made up of the same confused shifting matter as life. But none of these theories of immortality inspire me with confidence; the system of retributions and punishments makes little impression upon a judge well aware of the difficulties of judging. On the other hand, the opposite solution seems to one also too simple, the neat reduction to nothingness, the hollow void where Epicurus' disdainful laughter resounds.
>
> I try not to observe my own ending: this series of experiments conducted on myself continues the long study begun in Satyrus' clinic. So far the modifications are . . . external . . . I am what I always was; I am dying without essential change.

Perhaps only poetry can express this without becoming hopelessly entangled in certain resonances and effects.

We can only speak of death in terms of the other, since no one may speak of his *own* death, just as no one can speak of his *own* birth. Thus, paradoxically, of the two extremes circumscribing our lives, the fundamental conditions of birth and death, we cannot be conscious. Yet, in some way, *our* death is also familiar to us, at home with us, following us like a shadow or the guardian angel of childhood and popping up in our thoughts, unexpected and unbeckoned. Ungaretti (1932) wrote:

O sister of shadow,
The fiercer the light is, the more a thing of night,
You pursue me, death.
In a perfect garden
Innocent longing gave birth to you
And peace was lost,
Pensive death,
On your mouth.
Ever since that instant
I have heard you in the mind's flow
Probing distances,
You who copy the eternal one, but suffer.
Venomous mother of the ages
In the fear of the pulse
And of solitude,
Beauty tormented and laughing,
In the drowsing of the flesh
A fugitive dreamer,
Unsleeping athlete
Of our greatness,
When you have tamed me, say:
Through the misery of living men
Will my shade's flight be long?

Death, therefore, negates existence simply by imposing a limit.
In terms of everyday life, this means that every project can be
invalidated, all hopes dashed. It is as though the sense of our
every action were continually placed in question and the value
we give it drastically reduced by virtue of its precariousness. Although the idea of the transience of all earthly things may have
been instilled in us since childhood, we will all nevertheless
nourish certain long-range projects, forgetting—or pretending to
forget—the limit imposed by death. And that is as it should be,
because only through great expectations can our consciousness
freely expand. And it is perhaps just in that free expansion of
consciousness that our real destiny lies.

However, while that space reassures us and allows us to contemplate infinitely more vast horizons than the real limits of our
daily panorama, we will inevitably from time to time be aware
of a threat hanging over us—a presentiment, a vertiginous abyss
we avoid looking into. We will be forced to look into that abyss,
not just when someone close to us dies, but each time we expe-

rience distance separating us from a person we love; that vast chasm between us and all other human creatures, which not even love can fill. As Bousquet (1941) wrote:

> Death is the solitude of the person loved, the mist surrounding them which no tender word can penetrate. Death is pain and desperation in the same words which were once exaltation and happiness. Death is the tears shed upon hearing a word which once meant love.

Death is revealed to us as the impossibility to dissipate or penetrate that mist in order to reach those we love. It sometimes surprises us when, in the intensity of love, a word having a quite different intention calls up troubling resonances of *memento mori*. This sensation could describe the feeling of the character of Pulcinella when, at the acme of a joyous tarantella, he suddenly discovers hooded Death between his arms as his "lady."

Death touches us ever so lightly each day of our lives, in the thousand abandonments we experience or inflict, insinuating itself silently—but not for this less powerfully—in moments of happiness, spoiling our joy. Even if it were possible through some form of exorcism or lobotomy to keep that specter constantly at bay, we would in any case be overtaken by the terrible reality of death the moment it deprived us of a loved one. Once more, our only experience of death is as *spectators* in the death *of other human beings*, assisting, impotently, at the progressive and final reduction of the other's vital space as that person is transformed from life companion into phantasm. Life is progressive expansion, and death is its suffocation. The phantasms created by our witnessing this more or less expected syncope in those we love remain with us for the rest of our lives. The effects of this experience will never be canceled because no one can ever recompense us for our emotional investment in the person loved. The embraces, kisses, the physical pleasure we were never able to entirely return—everything, in a breath, in a moment, was gone. This event may be more painful than the trials of Job. Then, as orphans of the person loved, we will desire only silence and forgetfulness.

The death of the other implies immediate identification with a

common destiny (Antonelli 1981, 147). In one of the films of the
Taviani brothers, two elderly people ask to die at the same moment, introducing on stage those phantasms we mentioned. Two
individuals who have loved each other intensely must die together, because it would be impossible for two human beings
who have so deeply shared their psychic worlds to be separated.
Thus can certain "strange" suicides be explained, deaths in perfect succession; deaths which could be considered another form
of suicide.

Death's real betrayal lies in the fact that from the unconscious
point of view it seems utterly inconceivable and therefore
nonexistent. As the unconscious has no concept of the "no," it
therefore is deprived of the means of negating the indifference
of life's flow. No one, especially if her consciousness is inadequately differentiated, can coexist with the idea of death. Instead, she will unconsciously be convinced that she has sealed a
pact and thus gained immortality; otherwise, it would make no
sense to speak of betrayal. Another characteristic of the pain of
losing one we have loved is that it temporarily prevents any relationship which is not purely formal. This distance is what is
commonly described as someone being "closed in on oneself."
But, while the need of an emotional life is imperative, the need
for relationships is inborn, and on them depends our survival.
Our entire psychic life is based on the fact that we have had a
certain set of parents in a certain human environment which
slowly modeled our emotional and affective dimensions. Those
relationships, consequently, are our "containers," our mirrors,
and so indispensable to our psychic equilibrium that, when they
are absent, the individual is forced to take refuge in madness,
creating an internal interlocutor for the voices from within. Our
relationships with others make it possible for us to "contain" our
discomfort. When, for some reason, these relationships are interrupted, there is the *final confrontation*. Paradoxically, it is in
these extreme circumstances, when lies are no longer of any
use, that each of us must gather his strength and perhaps for the
first time look lucidly into his own interior life. The paradox
therefore lies in our being called upon to be strong in a moment
of extreme weakness. If birth is an interior-to-exterior movement, death is a volte-face bringing us back inside.

Nothing provides more compensation in life than the dimension of sentiment. If we were to be judged by a god (intent on pardon), that entity might pardon us for having loved—never for having thought—too intensely. Perhaps herein lies the origin of the concept of immortality; to counter the sensation of desolation and ending. Compensating for the desperation felt when faced with the possible end of all relationship is a concept which is extraordinary in the psychological context—rebirth, resurrection, metempsychosis—and which expresses the human attempt to reject definitive loss. Many religious and philosophical systems include the concept of birth after death in the form of the resurrection of the soul. Death is the final betrayal that ends every personal history; however, it is differentiated from all others in two ways. First, we can only submit to it, whereas—as regards the initial betrayal of birth—an active role can also be identified, *our* betrayal of the mother (the earliest abandonment or earliest instance of turning our back); second, it would frankly be difficult to see in *this* betrayal, through which life liquidates us once and for all, a vital, propulsive aspect, unless . . .

Unless, instead of considering death exclusively as a concrete and conclusive accident, we took into consideration the *idea* of death, the *awareness* of that unavoidable limitation of the duration of life. In this case, we might also become the betrayer—at which point, clearly, death must also provide access to the experience of transformation; that is, rebirth.

167

Twenty-One

Betrayal and Freedom

Nobody who finds himself on the road to wholeness can escape that characteristic suspension which is the meaning of crucifixion.
—Jung, *The Psychology of the Transference*

The theme of this book lies somewhere between two immense metaphysical loci. In one sense, betrayal can be a passive experience (and consequently the locus of death, *being betrayed*, the kiss of Judas) and in another, the experience of *being the betrayer*, exercising a transgressive will to override all prohibition. During our lifetime, we will inevitably assume both roles—alternately, betrayer and betrayed. Or, we could say that we assume both roles simultaneously, alternating with the shifting of scenes in the demonic drama of relationships in which we are both victim and persecutor. The complexity of the soul demands endless confrontation with our most hidden parts, just as becoming fully human requires the capacity to sustain a relationship with the polyhedric nature of the psyche, which can stupefy and disorient, at times even overwhelm. Being betrayed means being consigned to painful death, forced to experience in the first person the pain of abandonment and the loss of all familiar points of reference. But the symbolic, image-charged language of the psyche teaches us that every death is a rite of passage to newer forms of existence. As Jung wrote, developing the personality almost always requires a mortal *sacrificium*, and if we succeed in elaborating the experience of betrayal and mourning, the result can be transformation. As we know, Christ's crucifixion—as well as his redemption—was possible only because of the betrayal of an apostle. Jung, in *The Psychology of the Transference* (1946), wrote:

> Nobody who finds himself on the road to wholeness can escape that characteristic suspension which is the meaning of crucifixion. For he will infallibly run into things that thwart and "cross" him: first, the thing he has no wish to be . . . second, the thing he is not . . . and third, his psychic non-ego.

And so, our paths will always be strewn with betrayal, and not only for the purpose of annihilating us. For, while betrayal destabilizes, it also re-creates. The repetition of the ego's miraculous rediscovery of itself—according to Jung—is possible only if and when a breach is made in its temporal consistency and the everyday nature of its beliefs. Humanity must transcend its own limits if we are to discover new areas of ourselves.

Freud and Jung—along with Galileo, Bacon, Abelard, and Nietzsche—were perpetrators of the great betrayals of the cultural canons of their times. They were transgressors in a closed system of knowledge that excluded not only the possibility of challenge, but above all the possibility of discovering new orders of those mysterious worlds in which human beings are immersed. They paid for their rash temerity by becoming in their turn objects of betrayal. Posterity, however, amply rewarded their tenacity. For in that context, their betrayal was the negation of that which exists to the point of becoming crystallized, losing life and meaning. And what would the result of an idyllic existence, protracted into an uneventful eternity, have been for our forebears—if not to end the species at the very dawn of existence? In any case, that was not the turn taken by human destiny. If we observe the child during the first year of life, we see her pass through all the ancestral stages of human development, moving restless and curious among things and through them, becoming familiar with herself—going continuously toward ever newer goals, newer objects, further horizons of knowledge, abandoning and betraying the old toy for the new, the obsolete discovery for the successive marvel. It is a law of the psyche. The creative *daemon* of humanity, the longing for freedom and individuation, is expressed in the logic of betrayal.

Betrayal certainly is equivalent to dealing death, for it signifies betraying ourselves in what previously constituted our confidence and security. Faust went so far as to betray his own soul, delivering it to Satan in exchange for the possession of all knowledge. And then there is the tragic tale of Orpheus and Eurydice. The singing poet descended into the Underworld to gaze once more upon his departed love. There, he obtained permission to bring her back to the world of light and life—provided he did not turn back to look at her until they had completed the journey from Hades to the land of the living. Orpheus failed and thus betrayed his Eurydice, sealing her destiny and consigning her forever to the dark realm of death. Every one of us carries within us the memory of a Eurydice delivered to forgetfulness, a betrayed friendship, an unfaithful love. And perhaps within each of us, that significant event touched a lyrical chord, as it did in the poet Orpheus.

Joe Bousquet, a poet thoroughly betrayed by existence, was consigned to an eternal corporeal night. His marvelous *oeuvre* begins with that total and disarming betrayal (Bousquet 1941):

> I observed the truth from close quarters. I might say it rushed at me, shattering in me, enclosing in a strange aura the invalid I am, the invalid I become. . . . I am he whose life was interrupted early and who forced himself to believe in miracles in order to help things once more take on their normal course . . .
>
> I believed in miracles because that faith was all that was left to my instinct to survive. Now it seems as though the concept of luck marked my entire life, as though the chimeric form it assumed in order to appear to me had been fecundated by the very events reinforcing it. . . .
>
> Destiny had been fulfilled. There was nothing more for me to do than perpetuate within me, by day and by night, that light which made it possible for me to be distinguished from an infinity of others.

A paralyzed poet, relegated to his bed, illuminates us on the quality of an existence aimed at liberation from a betrayal that negated the desire for expansion, fulfillment—the betrayal of time, of love, of language, of forgetfulness. From the depths of that search which renders us all equal, Bousquet's words indicate the way to unveiling the betrayed truths concealed in our heart of hearts (ibid.):

> Until we put our own lives on the line, there will not be the strength necessary to draw from the shadow the basic traits of a character. We know instinctively which truth it is we must hold onto fast if we are to be saved from desperation.

When betrayal occurs, betrayer and betrayed become two sides of the same coin—just as, in the analytical setting, patient and analyst are continually called upon to test the certainties of their roles and values in order to permit unconscious reciprocal voices to emerge in a dialogue of souls. Only thus is the patient led to recognize in himself that image of the betrayer which—because of the projective distortion—he constantly sees reflected in the countenance of the other.

Actually, apart from the betrayals of life, it is the distorted logic of our compulsions and our own incapacities that are the real cause of our being trapped in those self-destructive situations inevitably destined to end in failure. As the saying goes, we are our own worst enemy—and the cruelest. And here, the analytical discourse on betrayal opens onto another register; the betrayal of ourselves. What patients going into analysis really suffer from is the betrayal of their more authentic ego, regardless of the infinity of other symptoms. She who suffers experiences an inner laceration, a collision between conscious needs and a nucleus of her personality which, because it is blocked, prevents those needs from being satisfied. Expressions such as "I'd like to get out of that situation, but I just can't" or "I'd like to work, but I'm unable to" are not infrequent. The repetition-compulsion—that perverse mechanism analyzed by Freud in *Beyond the Pleasure Principle*—is the unconscious compulsion to repeat the same errors, repeatedly taking a certain role and following the same negative and frustrating relationship pattern. The individual will persist in this perverse existence, on the road to self-betrayal. And yet, as that compulsion conceals, behind the obstinate repetition of the individual's own death, a desire to triumph over the interior demon, thus does betrayal represent an attempt at flight.

Obviously, my intention here is merely to attempt to preserve the paradoxical aspect; in other words, to avoid reducing to a single dimension a phenomenon so complex, so pregnant with contradiction, as every experience must be that the psyche colors and dispels, enlarges and mortifies. If people were free, they would have no need to betray. But, conversely, if people were not free, they could not betray. Betrayal is revolt, and every revolution is enclosed in the sphere of betrayal; every work of art that violates obsolete knowledge is a betrayal; every new discovery, every original intellectual movement, is betrayal. As we have seen, the parable of our lives proceeds in stages marked by this lacerating experience.

The word *betrayal* conceals the eternal struggle between Eros and Thanatos, life and death, beauty and deformity—in other words, everything around which human destiny revolves. It is always the desire for impossible completeness that arouses our nostalgia and urges the consciousness in the direction of newer destinations, which subsequently reveal the impossibility of definitive conclusion, but which all the same create distance between us and yesterday's dreams, from faces we have known and loved. It is, in other words, movement in the direction of betrayal. Nietzsche, that betrayer par excellence, spoke of an imminent and "ever more dangerous curiosity" which would lead him to betray his former faith, his intellectual tendencies, even his great friendship with Richard Wagner—who would become his mortal enemy. That betrayal was necessary.

As Nietzsche asked in *Human, All-Too-Human* (1878–1879), cannot all values be reversed? And do good and evil exist? And is God not merely an invention of the devil's perspicacity? And isn't everything, in the final analysis, false? And if we are deceived, are we not thus also deceivers? Must we not also be deceivers?

Thus has our discourse on betrayal come full circle, returning to its initial theme, that primary, original, and all-containing myth, around which not only psychoanalysis, but art, philosophy, and religion revolve: the myth of Paradise Lost. The memory of betrayal would seem to accompany and invest all thought—oriental and occidental—from the first human attempts to explain, through myth, the yearning for harmony and perfection, despite the incredulity experienced before a fearful and often hostile world. Humanity does not resign itself easily to nature's inscrutability or the great contradictions of existence and, in the great thirst for inner union, we will conceive all that frustrates that desire for harmony as nothing more than a cosmically absurd mistake.

Epilogue

Experience and Loss

Our first experience is loss.
—Lou Andreas-Salomé, *Looking Back,*
An Autobiography

The psychoanalytical experience of Lou Andreas-Salomé, whose very original autobiography we refer to here, began in 1911 after her meeting with Freud. In the opening of her book, she comments on the significance of the fact that our first experience should be one of loss. Shortly before, we had been whole, an indivisible entity, inseparable from all forms of existence—and then, we were suddenly forced to be born, becoming nothing more than a residual of that being and, from that moment on, we had to be on our guard against the imposition of new limitations, in order to survive in a world which increasingly spread out before us, that world into which we fell from cosmic plenitude.

And therefore, in a certain sense, our first experience was one of the past, a rejection of the present; the first "recollection," as it would be called subsequently, was at the same time a shock; disappointment for having lost what could be no more, but retaining at the same time a nagging awareness of it, with the certainty that it could be once more.

That attachment to what should still be is what creates the tension responsible for our titanic efforts to embrace existence, creating works that endure, despite the betrayal of time and history.

Fertile betrayal is at the same time our damnation; it is what condemns each of us to re-create ourselves in an endless

Promethean struggle, arousing the envy of the gods, but of others as well. For one who "betrays" thus will inevitably be the object of harsh, negative collective judgment, and conducting a life faithful to one's most authentic aspirations will always be stigmatized as betrayal. Something very similar occurs during the analytical process when a patient defensively resists transformation. And the reason for such resistance is that often, for a fragile ego, upsetting the precarious—if reassuring—status quo to create a newer equilibrium (inevitably considered dangerous) is impossible. The process of individuation, in fact, also involves betraying the expectations others have of us—expectations that can manipulate us, alienating us from our true nature.

Consequently, the patient may unconsciously negate his own psychological development because he fears its clearly destructive potential, because he fears betraying, which would repeat the primordial transgression of Adam and Eve against divine law. Psychoanalysis, as therapeutic technique, and even more so as knowledge, has from its origins been considered a discipline which reveals—"betrays"—old certainties by unveiling the unknown aspect of the known. Therefore, it should not surprise us that Freud—along with Copernicus and Darwin—was considered a subverter of a particular concept of humanity—the Cartesian concept—according to which each of us is totally identified with the "I think" of conscious processes. Freud discredited that simulacrum when he demonstrated that the conscious ego is nothing more than a buoy floating on the surface of the immense sea of the unconscious. In this way, he courageously unveiled the unsaid, revealing troubling shadows of repressed sexuality, death, and frustrated desire. In the same way, if we were to consider every phenomenon connected with the human universe (growth, love, creativity) together with its darker side (death), we would discover that what limits and betrays us may also be what defines and reveals us.

Bibliography

Abel, K. 1884. *Der Gegensinn der Urworte*. Lipsdig.

Accetto, T. 1641. *Della dissimulazione onesta* (Honest Dissimulation). Genoa: Costa and Nolan, 1983.

Adler, A. 1920. *The Practice and Theory of Individual Psychology*. Paterson, N.J.: Littlefield, Adams, 1963.

Alvarez, A. 1970. *The Savage God: A Study of Suicide*. London: Penguin, 1974.

Amery, J. 1976. *Hand an sich legen. Diskurs über den Freitod* (Committing Suicide). Stuttgart: Klett.

Andreas-Salomé, L. 1951. *Lebensruckblick* (Looking Back, An Autobiography). Frankfurt am Main: Insel Verlag, 1968.

Antonelli, F. 1981. *Per morire vivendo. Psicologia della morte*. Rome: Città Nuova Editrice, 1990.

Aristotle. *Etichs*. London: Penguin Classics, 1955.

———. *Nicomachean Ethics*. London: Penguin Classics.

Augustine. *De civitate Dei*. Harmondsworth: Penguin Books, 1972.

Balzac, H. de. 1829. *Physiologie du mariage*. Paris: Garnier-Flammarion, 1968.

Barthes, R. 1977. *A Lover's Discourse. Fragments*. London: Jonathan Cape, 1979.

Bataille, G. 1962. *Eroticism*. London: Marion Boyars Publishers, Ltd., 1987.

Bauderlaire, C. 1857. Flowers of evil. In *Selected Poems*. London: Penguin Books, 1975.

Beck, D. 1981. *Krankheit als Selbsteinlung*. Frankfurt am Main: Insel Verlag.

Benda, J. 1927–1958. *Il tradimento dei chierici*. Torino: Einaudi, 1976.

Bergonzi, M. 1990. La crescita e il tradimento. In *Revista di Psicologia Analitica* 42.

Berne, E. 1964. *Games People Play.* New York: Grove Press, Inc., 1964.

Blixen, K. 1981. *On Modern Marriage and Other Observations.* London: Fourth Estate, Ltd., 1987.

Bloch, E. 1975. *Experimentum mundi. Frage, Kategorien des Herausbringens, Praxis.* Frankfurt am Main: Suhrkamp Verlag.

Borges, J. L. 1944. *Ficciones.* Buenos Aires: Editorial Sur.

⸺. 1952. *Otras inquisiciones.* Buenos Aires: Editorial Sur.

Bousquet, J. 1941. *Traduit du silence.* Paris: Editions Gallimard.

Bowen, M. 1966. *Family Therapy in Clinical Practice.* Northvale, N.J.: Aronson, Jason Inc., 1978.

Bowen, M., and Kerr, M. 1971–1972. *Family Evaluation.* London: W.W. Norton and Co., Ltd., 1989.

Bozoky, E., ed. 1980. *Le livre secret des Cathares. Interrogatio Iohannis. Apocryphe d'origine bogomile.* Paris: Beauchesne.

Breger, L. 1989. *Dostoevsky: The Author as Psychoanalyst.* New York and London: New York University Press.

Brelich, A. 1969. Aristofane: commedia e religione. In *Il mito. Guida storica e critica,* M. Detienne, ed. Bari: Laterza, 1976.

Brentano, F. 1874. *Psychology from an Empirical Standpoint.* London: Routledge and Kegan Paul, 1973.

Bufalino, G. 1981. *Diceria dell'untore* (Rumors of the Plague Spreader). Palermo: Sellerio.

Calame, C. 1977. Les chœurs de jeunes filles en Grèce archaïque. Rome: Ateneo e Bizzarri, 420–429. [In *L'amore in Grecia,* Bari: Laterza, 1983.]

Campbell, D. A., ed. 1982. *Sappho Alcaeus.* In *Greek Lyric in Four Volumes,* vol. I. Cambridge, Mass.: Harvard University Press; London: William Heinemann.

Camus, A. 1942. *Le Mythe de Sisyphe.* Paris: Gallimard.

Cappelano, A. (André le Chapelain) 1980. *De Amore.* Milan: Guanda.

Carotenuto, A. 1987. *Eros and Pathos: Shades of Love and Suffering.* Toronto: Inner City Books, 1989.

⸺. 1989. Sulle ipotesi che sono a fondamento della terapia psicologica. In *Itinerari del pensiero junghiano,* P. Aite and A. Carotenuto, eds. Milan: Raffaello Cortina Editore.

⸺. 1990. *Le rose nella mangiatoia. Metamorfosi e individu-*

azione nell "Asino d'oro" di Apuleio. Milan: Raffaello Cortina Editore.

Castellana, F. 1990. L'analista e la relazione analitica. Una breve sintesi, pensando al tradimento. In *Rivista di Psicologia Analitica* 42.

Chiozza, L. A. 1986. *Perché ci ammaliamo. La storia che si nasconde nel corpo.* Rome: Borla, 1988.

Cicero, Marcus Tullius. *De natura deorum.* Harmondsworth: Penguin, 1972.

Clement of Alexandria. (Clemente Alessandrino.) *Stromati.* Turin: Ed. Paoline, 1985.

Cohen, A., ed. 1932. *Selections: Everyman's Talmud.* London: Kuperard Ltd., 1978.

David, C. 1971. *L'Etat Amoreux.* Paris: Payot.

Dickinson, E. *The Complete Poems of Emily Dickinson,* Thomas J. Johnson, ed. Boston and Toronto: Little, Brown and Co., 1960.

Di Meglio, D. 1990. *L'invisibile confine. Ermafroditismo e omosessualità.* Rome: Melusina Editrice.

Donne, J. 1603. *Biathanatos,* Ernest Sullivan, ed. London: Associated University Presses, 1984.

———. 1624. *Devotions upon Emergent Occasions.* New York and Oxford: Oxford University Press, 1987.

Dostoevsky, F. 1876. A gentle spirit. In *The Diary of a Writer.* Salt Lake City: Peregine Smith Books, 1985.

Dover, K. J. 1973. Sexual behaviour of the Greeks in the classic age. In *Arethusa* 6, 59–74. [*L'amore in Grecia,* C. Calame, ed. Bari: Laterza, 1983.].

———. 1978. *Greek Homosexuality.* London: G. Duckworth and Co., Ltd., 1987.

Edinger, E. F. 1986. *The Bible and the Psyche: Individuation Symbolism in the Old Testament.* Toronto: Inner City Books.

Eliot, T. S. 1963. *Collected Poems, 1902–1962.* London: Faber and Faber, 1974.

Elkaim-Sartre, A., ed. 1982. *Aggadoth du Talmud de Babylon.* Lagrasse, France: Verdier.

Erbetta, M. 1982. *Gli apocrifi del Nuovo Testamento. Vangeli. Testi giudeo-cristiani e gnostici.* Casale Monferrato: Marietti.

Falcolini, L. 1990. Il tradimento del corpo. In *Rivista di Psicologia Analitica* 42.

Filone of Alexandria. *La creazione del mondo. Le allegorie delle leggi*, Giovanni Reale, ed. Milan: Rusconi, 1978.

Forster, E. M. 1971. *Maurice*. New York: Norton.

Francis, C., and Goutier, F. 1985. *Simone de Beauvoir*. London: Mandarin, 1988.

Freud, S. 1908. Family romance. In *SE*, vol. 9. London: The Hogarth Press, 1959.

———. 1910. The antithetical meaning of primal words. In *SE*, vol. 11. London: The Hogarth Press, 1957.

———. 1912–1913. Totem and taboo. In *SE*, vol. 13. London: The Hogarth Press, 1955.

———. 1915–1917. Introductory lectures on psychoanalysis. In *SE*, vol. 15, 16, London: The Hogarth Press, 1963.

———. 1920. Beyond the pleasure principle. In *SE*, vol. 18. London: The Hogarth Press, 1955.

———. 1929. Civilization and its discontents. In *SE*, vol. 21. London: The Hogarth Press, 1961.

Fumagalli, V. 1990. *Solitudo carnis. Vicende del corpo nel Medioevo*. Bologna: Il Mulino.

Ganzerli, P., and Sasso, R. 1979. *La "rappresentazione anoressica." Contributo delle tecniche psicodiagnostiche allo studio dell'anoressia mentale*. Rome: Bulzoni.

Gibran, Kahlil. 1883–1931. *The Prophet*. New York: Knopf, 1923.

Graves, R. 1955. *The Greek Myths*. London: Penguin Books, 1960.

Hillesum, E. 1981. *Het verstoorde leven 1941–1943*. The Netherlands: De Haan-Unieboek B. V. Bussum.

Hillman, J. 1964a. *Suicide and Soul*. New York: Harper and Row.

———. 1964b. Betrayal. In Senex and Puer: An Aspect of Historical and Psychological Present. *The Guild of Pastoral Psychology* 128.

———. 1983. *Healing Fiction*. Barrytown, N.Y.: Station Hill Press.

Homer. *The Iliad*, Richmond Lattimore, tr. Chicago and London: The University of Chicago Press, 1979.

Hopcke, R. H. 1989. *Jung, Jungians, and Homosexuality*. Boston and Shaftesbury: Shambhala.

Hume, D. 1756. Sul suicidio (On Suicide). In *Opere filosofiche*, vol. 3. Bari: Laterza, 1987. English translation: *Moral and Political Philosophy*, H. D. Aiken, ed.

Isnardi Parente, M., ed. 1989. *Stoici antichi*. Turin: UTET.

Jaffé, A., ed. 1975. *Esperienza e mistero. 100 lettere*. Turin: Boringhieri, 1982.

Jung, C. G. 1912–1952. Symbols of transformation. In *CW*, vol. 5. Princeton, N.J.: Princeton University Press, 1956.

———. 1917–1943. On the psychology of the unconscious. In *Two Essays on Analytical Psychology. CW*, vol. 7. Princeton, N.J.: Princeton University Press, 1972.

———. 1923. Child development and education. In *CW*, vol. 17. New York: Pantheon Books, 1954.

———. 1925. Marriage as a psychological relationship. In *CW*, vol. 17. New York: Pantheon Books, 1954.

———. 1926–1946. Analytical psychology and education, three lectures. In *CW*, vol. 17. New York: Pantheon Books, 1954.

———. 1927–1931. Introduction to Wickes' "Analyses der Kinderseele." In *CW*, vol. 17. New York: Pantheon Books, 1954.

———. 1928. The relation between the ego and the unconscious. In *CW*, vol. 7. Princeton, N.J.: Princeton University Press, 1972.

———. 1929. Paracelsus. In *CW*, vol 15. Princeton, N.J.: Princeton University Press, 1971.

———. 1929–1957. Commentary on "The Secret of the Golden Flower." In *CW*, vol. 13. Princeton, N.J.: Princeton University Press, 1967.

———. 1934–1939. *Nietzsche's Zarathustra. Notes of the Seminar Given in 1934–1939*. Princeton, N.J.: Princeton University Press, 1988.

———. 1937. Is analytical psychology a religion? In *C. G. Jung Speaking. Interviews and Encounters*. William McGuire and R. F. C. Hull, eds. London: Pan Books, 1980.

———. 1942. Paracelsus as a spiritual phenomenon. In *CW*, vol. 13. Princeton, N.J.: Princeton University Press, 1967.

———. 1946. The psychology of the transference. In *CW*, vol. 16. Princeton, N.J.: Princeton University Press, 1966.

———. 1952. Answer to Job. In *CW*, vol. 11. Princeton, N.J.: Princeton University Press, 1969.

————. 1955–1956. *Mysterium Coniunctionis*. In *CW*, vol. 14. Princeton, N.J.: Princeton University Press, 1970.

————. 1961. *Memories, Dreams, Reflections*. New York: Pantheon Books, 1961.

Kierkegaard, S. 1834–1855. *Diary*. Peter Rohde, ed. New York: Philosophical Library, 1960.

Klein, M. 1959–1963. *Our Adult Word and Other Essays*. London: Heinemann Chemical Books, 1959–1960.

Kracauer, S. 1971. *Sull'amicizia*. Geneva: Marietti, 1989.

Kristeva, J. 1987. *Soleil Noir*. Paris: Gallimard.

La Rochefoucauld, F. de. 1665. *Maximes et Réflexions diverses*. Paris: Editions Gallimard, 1976.

Leclaire, S. 1971. *Demasquer le Real*. Paris: Edition Seuil.

Leopardi, G. *Tutte le opere*. 2 vol. Florence: Sansoni, 1976.

Leto, G., ed. 1966. *Ovidio. Le Eroidi*. Turin: Einaudi, 1977.

Levinas, E. 1971. *Totalité et infini*. Boekhandel en Vitgeversmaatschappiy: Martinus-Niyhoff Publishers.

————. 1972. *Humanism de l'autre homme*. Montpellier: Editions Fata Morgana.

Lichtenberg, J. 1983. *Psychoanalysis and Infant Research*. Hillsdale, N.J.: The Analytic Press.

Luther, M. 1566. *Basic Theological Writings*, Timothy Lull, ed. Minneapolis: Aubsburg Fortress Pubs., 1989.

Masters, E. L. 1914. *Spoon River Anthology*. New York: Macmillan Publishing Company, 1962.

Michaelstaedter, C. 1910. *Il dialogo della salute e altri dialoghi* (Dialogue Between Charles and Nadia). Milan: Adelphi, 1988.

Miller, A. 1981. *Du solist nicht merken: Variationen: über das Paradies-Thema*. Frankfurt am Main: Suhrkamp Verlag.

Milton, J. 1667. *Paradise Lost*, books VII–XII. Cambridge: Cambridge University Press.

Moliere 1665. *Don Juan*. Oxford: Oxford University Press, 1989.

Moor, P. 1989. Una ipocrisia psicoanalitica. In *Psicoterapia e scienze umane* 2.

Nelli, R., and Lavaud, R., eds. 1966. *Les Troubadours. Le trésor poétique de l'Occitanie*, vol. 2. Bruges: Desclée de Brouwer.

Nerval, G. de. 1852. *Les Chimères*, Norma Rinsler, ed. London: Athlone Press, 1973.

Neumann, E. 1953. The psychology of feminine development. In *Spring* 1959.

Nietzsche, F. 1878–1879. Human, all-too-human. In *CW*, vol. VI and VII. London: T. N. Foulis, 1910–1911.

Olievenstein, C. 1988. *Le non-dit des emotions*. Edition Odile Jacob.

Olivier, C. 1980. *Jocasta's Children: The Imprint of the Mother*, G. Craig, tr. London: Routledge, 1989.

Ovid. *Amores*, E. A. Barspy, ed. Bristol: Bristol Classical Press, 1979.

———. *Heroides*. A. Palmer, ed. Hildesheim, Germany: Gg Olms, 1967.

Paz, O. 1959. *El laberinto de la soledad* (Labyrinth of Solitude). Mexico: Fondo de Cultura Economica.

Philo of Alexandria. *Works of Philo: complete and unabridged*, C. D. Yonze, tr. Peabody, Mass.: Hendrickson Publishers, 1993.

Pindar. *The Odes*. London: Penguin Classics, 1969.

Plath, S. 1960. *Collected Poems*. New York: Harper Perennial, 1992.

———. 1975. *Letters Home*. Harper and Row Publishers.

Plato. *The Republic*. London: Penguin Classics, 1969.

———. *Symposium*. London: Penguin Classics.

Racugno, N., ed. 1989. *Conoscere i miti*. Turin: Thema Editore.

Rank, O. 1909. *The Myth of the Birth of the Hero*. New York: Robert Brunner, 1952.

———. 1912. The Incest Theme in Literature and Legend. Baltimore: John Hopkins University Press, 1991.

———. 1914. *The Double*, Harry Tucker, tr. Chapel Hill, N.C.: University of North Carolina Press, 1971.

———. 1922. *The Don Juan Legend*, David G. Winter, tr. Princeton, N.J.: Princeton University Press, 1975.

———. 1924. *The Trauma of Birth*. New York: Robert Brunner, 1952.

Rilke, R. M. 1910. *Notebooks of Malte*, J. Linton, tr. Oxford: Oxford University Press, 1984.

———. 1929. *Briefe an einen jungen Dichter*. Frankfurt am Main: Insel Verlag, 1929.

Sacchetti, F. *Il Trecentonovelle*. Turin: Einaudi, 1970.

Seneca. *Letters from a Stoic*, R. Campbell, tr. London: Penguin Classics, 1985.

Serrano, M. 1966. *C. G. Jung and Hermann Hesse. A Record of Two Friendships*. London: Routledge and Kegan Paul.

Shakespeare, W. *Richard II*. Middlesex: Penguin Books, 1967.

Socrates. *Paerdrus*. London: Penguin Classics.

Sophocles. *The Complete Plays of Sophocles*. New York: Bantam Books, 1967.

Stendahl. 1822. *De l'Amour*. Paris: Mongie.

Tanner, T. 1979. *Adultery in the Novel*. Baltimore: The John Hopkins University Press.

Theognis. Elegies. In *Hesiod*, Richard Caldwell, ed. Newburyport, Mass.: Focus Information Group, Inc., 1988.

Thomas, E. 1986. *Le viol du silence*. Paris: Éditions Aubier Montaigne.

Ungaretti, G. 1932. *106 poesie 1914–1960*. Milan: Mondadori, 1966.

Verde, J. B., and Pallanca, G. F. 1984. *Illusioni d'amore. Le motivazioni inconsce nella scelta del partner*. Milan: Raffaello Cortina Editore.

Vidal-Naquet, P. 1977. *Flavius Josephe ou du bon usage de la trahison*. Paris: Les Editions de Minuit.

Voltaire. 1764. *Philosophical Dictionary*. London: Penguin Classics, 1972.

———. *Candide*. London: Penguin Classics.

Wickes, F. G. 1927. *The Inner World of Childhood*. New York: Appleton Century-Crofts, Inc.

Wilde, O. 1905. *De Profundis*. London: Penguin Classics, 1973.

Wolff, H. 1975. *Jesus der Mann: die Gestalt Jesu in tiefenpsychologischer Sicht*. Stuttgart: Radius-Verlag Gmbh.

Yourcenar, M. 1951. *Memoirs of Hadrian*, Grace Frick, tr. Middlesex: Penguin Books, 1978.

———. 1957. *Fires*, Dori Katz, tr. London: Black Swan (Transworld Publishers Limited), 1985.

———. 1980. *Mishima*, A. Manguel, tr. New York: Farrar, Straus and Giroux, 1986.

Index